The Budapest Museum of Fine Arts

Edited and with a Preface
by Klára Garas

Contributors:
István Barkóczi, Brigitta Cifka, Andrea Czére, Ildikó Ember,
Éva Sz. Eszláry, Éva Nyerges, Ágnes Szigethy, János György Szilágyi,
Vilmos Tátrai, Zsuzsa Urbach, Edith Varga

CORVINA

Contents

Title of the Hungarian original: *Szépművészeti Múzeum*,
Corvina Kiadó, Budapest, 1985
English translation by Mária Steiner
Translation revised by Elisabeth West

©Klára Garas, 1985
Second edition
ISBN 963 13 3088 5

Colour plates:

KÁROLY SZELÉNYI: Egyptian Art, Classical Antiquities, Old
  Masters (1., 2., 3., 5., 6., 8., 9., 12., 13., 15., 16., 17., 22., 25.,
  26., 27., 29., 32., 33., 34., 36., 37., 38., 39., 40., 41., 45., 46.,
  47., 50., 51., 52., 53., 54., 57., 58., 60., 61., 62., 63., 64., 68.,
  69., 72., 73., 74., 76., 77., 78., 79., 80., 81., 82., 84., 85., 86.,
  88., 90.); European Sculpture, Prints and Drawings (2., 3.,
  4., 6., 7., 8., 10., 11., 12., 13., 14., 15.); Modern Art (1., 3.,
  4., 5., 6., 7., 8., 9., 10., 11., 13., 14., 15., 16.)
ALFRÉD SCHILLER: Old Masters (4., 7., 11., 14., 18., 19., 20.,
  21., 24., 28., 42., 43., 44., 48., 49., 55., 59., 65., 66., 71., 75.,
  83., 87., 89.); Prints and Drawings (1., 5., 9.); Modern Art
  (2., 12.)
LÁSZLÓ GYARMATHY: Old Masters (10., 23., 30., 31., 35., 56.,
  67., 70.)

Black-and-white reproductions: András Rázsó,
Mária Szenczi
Reproductions for the Introductory Section: Károly Szelényi
(pp. 8., 9., 15.), László Gyarmathy (upper picture, p. 9.),
MTI (pp. 6., 7., 12., 15.)
Photograph on the jacket by János Bakos
Designed by János Lengyel

Reproductions by M. Denis, O. Kokoschka, V. Vasarely
© 1985 by S.P.A.D.E.M., Paris
Reproductions by É. Béothy, P. Bonnard, M. Chagall,
A. Magnelli, G. Severini © 1985 by Cosmopress, Geneva

Printed in Hungary, 1990
Egyetemi Printing House, Budapest

Preface

The Budapest Museum of Fine Arts is considered one of the great museums of Europe. The variety of its holdings, its historical continuity and the large number of masterpieces have ensured the museum a secure place among the major art collections. Through personal experience and publications, it has been known for many years among artists, art historians and art lovers; now, however, thanks to the large number of visitors and faster communication, it has drawn more general interest.

Unlike a great many museums in Europe, the foundation of the Budapest Museum of Fine Arts is not linked to royal or princely art holdings but to the Hungarian national revival. Its present shape, too, dates back only to 1906, when the museum opened its doors, though its holdings and structure reflect almost two centuries of collecting work and cultural policy. The museum was born of the merger of a number of collections, galleries and foundations, and its holdings and fields of collecting have not only grown through the years, but also undergone change. For a long time it also housed Hungarian art works, but the speedy growth of the two major collections soon called for a separation of domestic and foreign art. In this way the Hungarian National Gallery was founded in 1957. Located in Buda Castle, it now unites all the treasures of Hungarian art, while since 1974—in accordance with its aim as expressed in the year of its foundation "to represent a link between the past and the future, to preserve the most worthwhile artistic traditions, to provide a foundation for progress, and be an eternal source of good taste and inspire a better knowledge of art"—the Museum of Fine Arts has dedicated itself exclusively to collecting and exhibiting foreign art.

KLÁRA GARAS
FORMER GENERAL DIRECTOR
AND MEMBER OF THE HUNGARIAN ACADEMY OF SCIENCES

History of the Museum and the Collections

The Museum of Fine Arts, opened in 1906, united the holdings of several large national art collections. Its history is inseparable from the history of these collections—the foundation of the National Museum and its collections, the Jankovich and Pyrker galleries, the collection of paintings in Buda Castle, the Esterházy gallery, the Ipolyi Collection, and the foundation of the National Picture Gallery.

1458–1490. In Hungary, the Renaissance was marked by the rule of King Matthias Corvinus, who built up a considerable collection of art treasures and a library of European renown in his royal castle in Buda. He was given numerous paintings and sculptures by Italian princes: Lorenzo Medici sent him bronze reliefs by Verrocchio, and Lodovico Sforza presented him with a *Madonna* by his "best painter", presumably Leonardo, as the prince had heard that Matthias "*se delecta molto di belle pitture*". The royal collection was also enriched by works commissioned from Italian masters, some of whom the king had invited to Buda.
Contemporary records reveal how much these treasures were appreciated; unfortunately, they shared the tragic fate of the Bibliotheca Corviniana during the period of political unrest following the king's death, and later during the Turkish occupation of Buda, when they were dispersed and many of them were destroyed.

1721. Pál Esterházy, the Prince Palatine (1635–1712) laid the foundation of the Esterházy Collection, which was housed in the family palaces at Frakno and Kismarton. In his will, the prince made special reference to various pieces of fine workmanship, family portraits and certain paintings in the spirit of the traditional *Kunstund Wunderkammer*. The Kismarton inventory of 1721 lists some 800 paintings, unfortunately without naming the painters or describing the works in any detail. Although some of these treasures may have been included in the Esterházy Collection which finally came to the Museum of Fine Arts, we have no proof for such identification.

1781. Pozsony, Castle (now Bratislava, Czechoslovakia) was the official residence of Archduchess Maria Christina and her husband Archduke Albert. The paintings had been provided by Queen Maria Theresa in 1770, but in 1781, when the couple moved to the Netherlands, some of the paintings were taken back to Vienna and, according to another list drawn up in the same year, were replaced by other pictures. Later, from 1784 onwards, the pictures were transferred to the Royal Castle in Buda, where in the first half of the nineteenth century, some of them were hung in the Palatine's apartments.

1784. The Esterházy Collection was brought together and displayed by Prince Miklós Esterházy (the Magnificent) (1714–1790) in the gallery of his newly built palace at Eszterháza (now Fertőd). According to contemporary descriptions, the collection comprised some 350 exquisite paintings. His grandson Prince Miklós (1765–1833) enriched the family collection with paintings and drawings bought during his travels in Italy and with the help of Italian and Viennese agents. Around 1800 he acquired masterpieces from the famous collections in Naples and Rome, owned by, among others, the Princes Borghese, Doria Pamphili and Barberini. These included Correggio's *Virgin and Child with an Angel (Madonna del Latte)*, Bronzino's *The Adoration of the Shepherds*, Claude Lorrain's *Villa in the Roman Campagna* and Raphael's *Portrait of the Young Pietro Bembo*.

1802. The first Hungarian public collection, founded by Count Ferenc Széchényi and supported by public contributions, was primarily intended for the exhibition of relics from Hungarian history, but it also served to house works of art. The gallery was founded by various bequests and donations. The acquisitions were exhibited in the new neo-Classical building of the National Museum designed by Mihály Pollack.

1804. The Esterházy princes now transferred their collection from the family castles in Kismarton and Eszterháza to their palace in Pottendorf (Lower Austria), where it was enlarged by new acquisitions and a curator was appointed, the Vienna engraver Josef Fischer. In 1812 the threat of Napoleon's approaching armies forced the family to remove the collection to their palace at Laxenburg. It was there that the first printed catalogue, edited by J. Fischer, was issued in German and French. In

1813 the collection was taken to Vienna and housed in the newly purchased Kaunitz Palace in the Mariahilf district. Until the middle of the nine-

J. Fischer's wash drawing of Prince Miklós Esterházy

teenth century the collection, by then open to the public, was one of the chief attractions of Vienna.

1810. In return for an annuity, Prince Miklós Esterházy acquired, in Paris, the famous collection of drawings owned by Cavaliere Antonio Cesare Poggi, whose family came from Parma. The purchase included Leonardo's two world-famous red chalk drawings, studies for the *Battle of Anghiari*, Raphael's *Psyche*, seven Rembrandt studies, and drawings by Nicolas Poussin and Claude Lorrain.

1819. In London Prince Pál Esterházy bought twenty-two pictures from the collection of Edmund Bourke, Danish ambassador to Spain.

1821. The remainder of the Bourke Collection, comprising twenty-six canvases, was bought from Bourke's widow in Paris. Bourke had bought the Italian and Spanish masterpieces by Tintoretto, Tiepolo, Murillo and Alonso Cano during the Napoleonic wars in Spain. These works (together with the pictures by Ribera and Goya), bought from the famous Viennese Kaunitz Collection, provided the foundation of the important and comprehensive Spanish collection at present in Budapest.

1832–36. During these years the National Museum acquired the works of art in possession of Miklós Janko-

vich, a noted collector in Pest. Apart from ancient Graeco-Roman and Hungarian historical relics, the acquisitions included valuable paintings and sculptures by Hungarian and other artists, for example several important mediaeval German panel paintings, Jacopo Tintoretto's *Portrait of a Man*, Giovanni Domenico Tiepolo's *God, the Father* and Andrea Pisano's statue of the *Virgin and Child*. All these treasures from the National Museum are now in the Museum of Fine Arts.

1836. The bequest from János László Pyrker, Archbishop of Eger, comprised one hundred and ninety-two paintings. Most of them he had purchased between 1820 and 1827 in Italy, when he was Patriarch of Venice. In 1846 the paintings, among them outstanding works by Italian, Netherlandish and German masters, were displayed in the new building of the National Museum. In the same year the first printed catalogue (edited by the curator, Gábor Mátrai) was also issued. The Pyrker Collection includes works of great beauty, for instance Gentile Bellini's famous *Portrait of Caterina Cornaro, Queen of Cyprus*, Giorgione's *Portrait of a Man* (believed to be Antonio Broccardo), Veronese's *Allegory of Venice*, Giovanni Battista Tiepolo's *The Virgin with Six Saints* and Memling's *Crucifixion*.

1848. Lajos Kossuth, the governor of Hungary during the War of Independence, transferred seventy-eight pictures from the residence of the former President of the Chamber into public domain, to be housed in the National Museum. Formerly these pictures were in Buda Castle, where they adorned the halls. They were chosen by Maria Theresa for the decoration of the royal apartment first in Pozsony and later in Buda Castle. In the seventeenth century some of them were in Archduke Leopold Wilhelm's famous collection, housed first in Brussels and later in Vienna. These came from the most noted Italian and English collections of the day and included works of great value such as Lorenzo Lotto's *The Sleeping Apollo and the Muses*, Dürer's *Portrait of a Man*, and Palma Vecchio's *Bust of a Youth* and *Bust of a Girl*. The paintings left in Buda Castle were sold at auction in 1856 by the court authorities. Some of these paintings, identifiable by the collector's mark, were sold at auctions and have been acquired recently to enrich still further the Museum of Fine Arts (for instance, *The Daughters of Lycomedes* by Quellinus, and Gentileschi's *Jael and Sisera*.)

1865. The collection was by now world-famous and in transferring it to Pest, Prince Esterházy was responding to public demand. Two years later, financial difficulties prompted Prince Miklós to offer the collection for sale to the Hungarian state.

1867. The paintings of the Esterházy Collection housed at the palace of Pottendorf were sold at an auction. Through Hungarian collections, some of these fine paintings (by Solimena, Dietrich, Droochsloot, Doyen) eventually found their way into the Museum of Fine Arts.

1870. In December the Hungarian state bought (for 1,300,000 forints) the entire Esterházy Collection, consisting of 637 paintings, some 3,500 drawings and 51,000 prints. This acquisition, made on behalf of the Hungarian nation, forms the nucleus of the collection at present in the Museum of Fine Arts. The acquisition brought into public domain such treasures as Raphael's *The Esterházy Madonna* and his *Portrait of the Young Pietro Bembo*, Correggio's *Virgin and Child with an Angel (Madonna del Latte)*, Veronese's *Crucifixion*, Tiepolo's *St. James the Greater*, Rembrandt's *The Old Rabbi*, *Mucius Scævola before Porsenna* by Rubens and Van Dyck, and canvases by Ribera, Murillo and Goya.

1871. By taking the Esterházy Collection into public ownership, the National Picture Gallery was founded and for want of a separate building, it was housed in a gallery of the Academy of Sciences. Gyula Hári's watercolours from 1904 show us how the gallery was arranged.

1872. Bishop Arnold Ipolyi was one of the pioneers of art historians in Hungary and his gift to the National Picture Gallery consisted of sixty-four valuable paintings by Old Masters, mainly early Italian, German and Hungarian panels. Most of the pictures originated from the collection of the painter Johann Anton Ramboux, which was auctioned in Cologne in 1869. Some of the Austrian and German panels had come from the Wiener-Neustadt collection of the painter Blasius Höfel, while the Hungarian paintings Ipolyi had bought when he was Bishop of Besztercebánya. The Ipolyi Gift included an altarpiece by Spinello Aretino, another by Ambrogio Lorenzetti, works by Giovanni di Paolo, Sassetta and Sano di Pietro, and *Thalia*, an extremely valuable work by Michele Pannonio.

1875. In order to present European art in one place, the art holdings of the National Museum (from the Jankovich, Pyrker, and other collections) were merged with the holdings of the National Picture Gallery. In 1884 Károly Pulszky was appointed director and under his custodianship the National Picture Gallery flourished. The collection was enlarged by purchases of important works such as Piombo's *Portrait of a Man*, Gerard David's *The Nativity*, Barend van Orley's *Portrait of Emperor Charles V* and some northern Italian frescoes. Pulszky also began to build up the relatively poor collections of classical antiquities and sculptures. By the end of the century, however, lack of space prevented further development. Adequate premises had to be found, and after much debate it was decided to establish a new institution, the Museum of Fine Arts.

1896. A law to "establish a National Museum of Fine Arts, with the provision of an adequate building raised on a suitable site to house its collections" was passed at the millenary session of the Parliament, celebrating the one thousandth anniversary of the establishment of Hungary. Of the 3,200,000 forints allocated for the project, 1,200,000 were intended for the building. The site at the end of the present-day Népköztársaság útja, was donated by the capital city free of charge. The plans included the erection of an imposing group of sculptures in the square.

1898. In September, tenders were invited and an international selection committee commissioned Albert Schickedanz and Fülöp Herzog to draw up the final designs. Construction began in the summer of 1900 and was completed in 1906.

1901. István Delhaes, a Hungarian painter living in Vienna, bequeathed a collection he amassed for several decades to the National Museum. This included a wealth of antiquities and some notable graphic works, among them the splendid series of studies and sketches by eighteenth-century Italian, Austrian and German masters (Gaspare Diziani, Paul Troger and Franz Anton Maulbertsch).

1906. The Museum of Fine Arts was opened in the presence of the Emperor and King, Francis Joseph. The huge complex of buildings incorporated a variety of architectural styles, as it was considered appropriate to Revivalist architecture. In the groundfloor galleries plaster casts of statues from all periods indicated the development of sculpture through the ages. In the upstairs galleries and cabinets, paintings were displayed. One gallery was reserved for prints and drawings.

1908, 1913. The collection of a German archaeologist, Paul Arndt, was bought to provide the basis for a Department of Classical Antiquities, which thereby acquired an international reputation.

1912. Count János Pálffy's Bequest enriched the Museum with 121 valuable works by old masters and 56 nineteenth-century works. The Pálffy Collection was established in the second half of the nineteenth century and included such gems as Titian's *Portrait of the Doge Marcantonio Trevisani*, Veronese's *Portrait of a Man*, Boltraffio's *The Lodi Madonna*, Petrus Christus's *Virgin and Child*; also works by Luca Giordano, Guercino, Jacob Ruisdael, Adriaen van Ostade and David Teniers the Younger.

1914. István Ferenczy's Bequest was bought from his heirs. István Ferenczy (1792–1856) was an eminent Hungarian neo-Classical sculptor, who had acquired most pieces of his collection in the early years of the nineteenth century, mainly in Rome (1818–24). The collection consisted of about eighty-three sculptures and included priceless treasures from the Italian Renaissance, such as Andreas

Riccio's bronze sculpture *The Rape of Europa*, the *Putto with Dolphin* from Verrocchio's workshop, and above all the famous equestrian bronze statuette attributed to Leonardo. In 1845 Ferenczy had offered these works for sale to the National Museum but his offer met with no response, and after his death the collection remained forgotten and unknown, in store in his studio at Rimaszombat.

1921. Donation of El Greco's *Mary Magdalene* by Marcell Nemes, a Hungarian collector living in Munich.
Five other important El Grecos and several outstanding relics of European painting (like *The Artist and his Family* and the *Portrait of Huldenberg* by Kupetzky, and *Friars at Lunch* by Magnasco) in possession of the Museum also came from his collection, some of them by way of Lipót M. Herzog.

1922. Donation by Jenő Boross, a collector of Hungarian extraction living in New York. This valuable gift included Jacopo Bassano's *Christ Collapses under the Cross*, Luis Tristán's signed altar wing *The Adoration of the Magi*, Langetti's *Joseph in Prison Interpreting Dreams* and Juan Carreño da Miranda's representative work, *St. James the Greater Conquering the Moors*.

1934. Under the Venice Agreement signed in 1932, several valuable works were sent to the Hungarian National Museum and the Museum of Fine Arts by way of compensation for Hungarian works of art taken to Austria. These include two wings of Memling's triptych and Tintoretto's *Hercules Expelling the Faun from Omphale's Bed*.
In the same year, Pál Majovszky, ministerial counsellor (1871–1935), donated his collection of drawings to the Museum. He had acquired most of the two hundred and fifty-nine drawings in Paris with the help of the eminent art historian Simon Meller. They include drawings by nineteenth- and twentieth-century masters, sketches and studies by Manet, Degas, Renoir and Cézanne, one of the finest being Delacroix's famous gouache: *Horse Frightened by Lightning*. Majovszky had already donated a valuable collection of prints to the Museum in 1914.

1944. The museum suffered heavy losses and damage. In the last phase of the war the director of the Museum, whose sympathies were with the fascists, made hurried plans to remove the valuable works to Germany. During the bombardment, some of the treasures were left at Szentgotthárd, near the Hungarian border, and these were taken back to the Museum in the summer of 1945. Many of them were seriously damaged by careless transport and storage. However, most of the works of art reached Germany, and their whereabouts remained unknown for a time.

Gyula Háry's watercolour of the exhibition rooms of the former National Picture Gallery

scholarly research, educational projects, classification and publications. For a time this progress was halted during the First World War and the post-war years of financial hardship. Nevertheless, in the years between the two world wars important additions were made to the Departments of Sculpture, Prints and Drawings, and Modern Art, such as the French drawings from the Majovszky Collection.

In the Second World War, however, the Museum was seriously damaged, and the very existence of the institution was threatened. The main staircase was hit by a bomb, and the glass roofs were completely destroyed. In the last months of the war, the fascists hastily and carelessly loaded the most valuable works from each department, that is, the greater part of the entire content of the museum, and took them to Germany. These were only gradually retrieved during 1946 and 1947 when many works were found in a greatly damaged condition. Still worse, a number of paintings were lost or destroyed during the war.

In the post-war years, the prime task was to repair the building, restore the damaged works and prepare exhibitions. The first temporary exhibition was arranged in 1946, and by 1949 the Gallery of Old Masters had been rearranged and was opened to the public. In the general postwar reorganization of museums, several major collections were allotted to the Museum of Fine Arts.

There followed systematic purchases and a spectacular development of various collections; for example the Departments of Egyptian Art and of Classical Antiquities now had the means to exhibit their collections on a broad historical basis. The works in the Department of Sculpture were almost doubled, and a policy was evolved for the establishment of a large collection of modern art.

For some years the Museum continued to house Hungarian art as well. Early relics of Hungarian art and works preserved formerly in the National Museum's Gallery, the former Art Gallery or the Budapest City Gallery, together constituted a considerable collection of Hungarian works which was further augmented by regular purchases and donations. The Museum proved insufficient for the display and storage of this material. Therefore in 1957 an independent Hungarian National

Gallery was established—an institution destined to collect and display works of Hungarian art dating from the earliest times to the present day. Thus a clear dividing line was drawn between the fields of activity of the two institutions. The Museum of Fine Arts is now dedicated exclusively to the collection, exhibition and study of foreign works of art.

The number of works preserved in the Museum is over 100,000. They are divided among six major departments: the Department of Egyptian Art, the Department of Classical Antiquities, the Gallery of Old Masters, the Department of European Sculpture, the Department of Modern International Art and the Department of Prints and Drawings. The finest works of each collection are permanently on view, arranged in chronological order. The lesser-known works and as yet unrestored works are in storage, though some of them are displayed temporarily.

The permanent exhibitions of Egyptian Art and of Classical Antiquities, a special collection of Italian fountains and frescoes, a collection of nineteenth- and twentieth-century sculpture and a display of contemporary works can be found on the ground floor. The Gallery of Graphic Art, the library and a lecture hall are also on the ground floor. The Gallery of Old Masters and the nineteenth-century paintings of the Department of Modern Art can be seen on the first floor. Baroque sculptures are housed on the next level, while the medieval and Renaissance sculptures are displayed in the galleries on the second floor. Temporary exhibitions are arranged in some of the halls, especially in the downstairs galleries. From six to ten such exhibitions are mounted every year, the works being selected from Hungarian collections arranged thematically or chronologically, as well as displays of works from museums abroad. The Museum has presented treasures from the Dresden Gallery, the Leningrad Hermitage and the Pushkin Museum of Moscow, nineteenth- and twentieth-century French paintings from Paris and English portraits from London, works from Mexico and Cuba, Thracian treasures from Bulgaria, and a selection or works under the title "The Birth of Rome". The exhibitions entitled the "Masterpiece of the Month" draw attention to recent

acquisitions, important anniversaries, or the completion of some major work of restoration.

Egyptian and Classical Antiquities

When the Museum was founded there was no plan for a Department of Antiquities. Instead it was proposed that the plaster copies of Greek and Roman statues, previously housed in the Hungarian National Museum, should be exhibited in the new museum, and that further purchases of casts should be made. The halls on the ground floor were adequate for this purpose. The collection of copies consisted of over 400 items. They were exhibited first in 1912, and again in a new arrangement in 1923. The copies remained on view until the Second World War, when many of them were seriously damaged. The surviving copies were considered to be worth retaining for scholarly and educational purposes, though not in the Museum of Fine Arts. The Kuny Domokos Museum of Tata has taken over the plaster copies and exhibited the collection in a completely new arrangement.

It was only after the opening of the Museum that the idea of collecting genuine antiquities emerged. It was due to the initiative of Antal Hekler that the Museum purchased a collection of 135 Greek, Italian and Roman marble statues, and later on, some time before the First World War a collection of 650 terracotta statuettes from Paul Arndt in Munich. From that time on there were regular purchases of classical statues up till 1922, but this period was followed by some 25 years when there were virtually no acquisitions of antiquities with the sole exception of an Attic stele with three figures, bought in 1928. But a new law passed in 1934 brought about a favourable change in the history of these collections: it allocated the Museum of Fine Arts all relics of Mediterranean antiquity (apart from those excavated in Hungary). This meant that the antiques donated to or bought by Hungarian collections, first and foremost the departments of the Hungarian National Museum, which grew into institutions in their own right, especially the Museums of first step was the reallocation of Ethnography, Applied Arts and Eastern Asiatic Art, were now incorporated with the holdings of

the Museum of Fine Arts. The Egyptian antiquities, which resulted in an antique statuary collection and the formation of the Egyptian Collection, which was exhibited in 1939. The reallocation of other material was largely curtailed by the Second World War, but after 1947, the varied relics of other Mediterranean cultures also reached the Museum, thus putting an end to the dominance of statuary. Since then relics of ancient Near Eastern, Egyptian, Greek, Italian and Roman art have been regularly purchased, and the last three decades saw the acquisition of a good many private collections and objects from provincial museums (mainly those that were unsuitable for local history exhibitions). Relics to fill gaps in the collections were bought in Egypt in 1959, and others were acquired in the following years through exchanges. By 1958 the Department of Egyptian Art had become autonomous and in 1964 it acquired, for the first time in the history of the Museum, finds from the eighth to the eleventh centuries A.D., which came from Hungarian excavations at Abdallah Nirqi in Nubia.

In fact, the Department of Egyptian Art is the only one in the Museum to possess works originating directly from excavations. Financed by the Hungarian Fülöp Back, a Polish Egyptologist, T. Smolenski, received a Hungarian commission in 1907 to collect fragments of reliefs from a temple erected by Ptolemy I at Sharuna (which has since been destroyed). Later on he unearthed several painted wooden mummy coffins from the Ptolemaic period at the Gamhud burial site. The Department of Classical Antiquities also cherishes some items that were unearthed by Hungarians—not always with scholarly methods: it was for instance Hungarian volunteers fighting with Garibaldi who, in 1861 near Rionero on the slopes of Vulture Hill, unearthed vases and terracotta statuettes which were in all probability dedicated in an Italic sanctuary. Another collection of Cypriote and eastern Greek pottery came from the excavations conducted in the 1860s on Cyprus by Count Ferenc Zichy, the Hungarian consul in Constantinople at that time. A number of Corinthian vases were acquired by Béla Gerster, one of the engineers in charge of the construction of the Corinth canal.

The origin of some other pieces,

mainly those acquired as part of the Arndt Collection, is no less interesting. Some come from ancient palaces in Italy (the Palazzo Grimani in Venice, the Palazzo Farnese and Palazzo Odeschalchi in Rome), while others, equally important, come from private collections which in the course of time have been dispersed (sculptures from the Grimani and the Tiepolo-Nani Collections in Venice, the Nelidow Collection in Constantinople, Adolf Furtwängler's Collection, as well as some Athenian red-figure vases from the second collection made by Sir William Hamilton and that of Count Franz von Lamberg).

It is, however, the history of Hungarian collecting from the eighteenth century to the present day that is most clearly demonstrated by the holdings in these two departments. They include items from virtually all the major Hungarian collections, from specimens collected by Mihály Viczay in the eighteenth century to all the antiquities collected by Hungarians ever since, such as the especially valuable collections of Jankovich, Fejérváry and Pulszky and the bronze sculptures collected by István Ferenczy. An important collection of Etruscan objects was acquired by the painter Antal Haán in the 1850s in Rome, Count Sándor Apponyi collected Greek vases in the late nineteenth century, István Delhaes the painter acquired bronze items at the turn of the century in Vienna, and Bonifác Platz collected relics in Egypt around the same time. All these collections have been transferred to the museum practically in their entirety. We should not forget about the Beőthy Collection either, which was taken to Uppsala but the Museum managed to buy many of its Egyptian pieces (along with some other objects).

The history of these two departments has determined to a large extent both the strong points and the shortcomings of the collections. The opportunities available for collecting, and the personal preferences of the collectors left their mark on them. The Department of Egyptian Art owns a few items of outstanding significance from each period of Egyptian sculpture. The statues from the Middle Kingdom are best represented by the upper part of a diorite statue of a pharaoh. The New Kingdom is best characterized by a limestone portrait of a man—one of the most remarkable works in the Depart-

ment. The Late Period is splendidly represented by the life-size kneeling limestone figure of Prince Shoshenq of the Twenty-second Dynasty, originating from Memphis. There is a very fine series of stelae; the earliest dates back to the time of the Old Kingdom. The New Kingdom and the Late Period are also extensively represented. This further collection is augmented by a memorial stele raised by Noferhaut and a stele painted on wood from the Ptolemaic period.

Another exquisite group of objects consists of painted coffins for mummies. Apart from the already mentioned Gamhud specimens, there are four coffins found at Deir el-Bahri (originally made for the Theban priests of Amon around 1000 B.C.), a coffin made for a priest of Monthu during the rule of the Twenty-second Dynasty, and another one dating from the early Roman period. There is also a small coffin from the Roman period. Its lid is carved in the form of the mummy of the funerary god Sokar, and it holds a grain mummy with the silver mask of Osiris over his face. Equally worthy of mention are the wooden figurines of servants dating from the First Intermediate Period, the wooden figurine of a priestess of the New Kingdom, the soapstone figurines of the two baboons of the god Thoth from the Ptolemaic era, a fine series of bronze statuettes of gods dating from the New Kingdom to the Ptolemaic period, and a few late sculpture moulds. A variety of Predynastic clay dishes, inscribed ushabtis, scarabs and amulets, a few items that deserve special attention such as a fragment of a papyrus stroll with mythological scenes from the Twenty-first Dynasty, and a necklace from the time of the Ptolemies, which consists of 36 gold figures of the goddess Thoueris make the collection complete.

Objects from the time of the Ptolemies and the Roman period, a few outstanding relics of Alexandrian marble sculpture, fine specimens of stucco mummy masks and mummy portraits painted on wood, nearly 300 terracotta statuettes from Graeco-Roman Egypt and a small Coptic collection which includes some notable painted clay vessels, bone carvings and textiles with figural patterns complement the Egyptian Collection (all of them belonging to the Department of Classical Antiquities).

Apart from the Cypriote collec-

tion mentioned already and the Punic pottery purchased in Sicily and North Africa, the Department of Classical Antiquities contains relics of Greek, Etruscan and Roman art. The most valuable of these are the statues acquired as part of the Arndt Collection and items from the Hungarian National Museum. From among the most outstanding works we should mention the archaic torso of a youth from Perinthos, relics of Athenian funerary sculpture from the fourth century B.C. (including the stele with three figures mentioned above and the torso of a monumental, draped male figure from Velanideza), the early Hellenistic figure of a girl known as the *Budapest Dancer,* and among the Roman copies, a recently acquired torso of Polykleitos' *Doryphorus,* portraits of writers and philosophers, and a small copy of the *Tyche* of Antioch. Within the Italic and Roman material mention must be made of the fragment of a historical relief dating back to the third century B.C. and coming from Lecce, a Capuan terracotta *Niobid,* the *Actium Relief,* and a series of Roman busts. Of the sculptures from the provinces of the Roman empire worthy of special mention are the portrait of a philosopher from Asia Minor, a sarcophagus depicting hunting scenes dating from the third century A.D., the work of an Athenian workshop from Salona, and a series of Macedonian and Phrygian stelae. Among architectural relics a Corinthian capital came to the Museum from Ephesus, and six Corinthian pilaster capitals from the Roman forum of Brescia.

The Collection contains more than 1,000 terracotta statuettes including many items from Attic, Boiotian and Eastern Greek workshops (all date back to the Archaic Period), from Tarentum (from the fifth and fourth centuries B.C.), and from workshops in Asia Minor, Myrina and Smyrna (from the Hellenistic age). Among the bronze objects it is principally the vases that deserve special mention, the *Grimani Jug* in particular. The series of Attic black-figure vases begins with an amphora by Exekias, that of the red-figure ones with the kylix (cup) by the Andokides Painter. Both series include works by noted painters ranging from the black-figure Swing Painter through the Brygos and Geras Painter to the Meleagros Painter of the fourth century B.C. The collection offers a practically

complete picture of vase painting of the fourth century B.C. in the Greek workshops in southern Italy (Apulia, Lucania, Campania, Paestum and Sicily).

Among the relics of the cultures of ancient Italy, we can find a small bronze statuette of a male figure from the ninth or eighth century B.C., the bucchero, the geometric, the black- and the red-figure vases of the Etruscan collection (including two pieces by the Micali Painter), a varied series of votive sculptures from Etruscan and other workshops in Italy and various types of archaic painted terracotta antefixes from Campania. There are special collections of Roman glass and lamps, and in a comprehensive selection of gems there are some interesting specimens from Graeco-Phoenician, archaic Greek and Etruscan workshops.

Old Masters

The Gallery of Old Masters is the most widely known section of the Museum, attracting the largest number of visitors. The nucleus of the collection comes from the Jankovich, the Pyrker, the Esterházy and the Ipolyi Collections, formerly housed in the National Museum and the National Picture Gallery. These collections, amassed during the eighteenth and nineteenth centuries, had a lion's share in shaping the character of the Gallery and determined the course of its development. The historical and geographical circumstances, the taste of the aristocrats and church dignitaries led to the preference for Italian painting. The collection of Miklós Jankovich, the bequest made by János László Pyrker, Archbishop of Eger, the pictures from Buda Castle and the Esterházy Collections contributed to the formation of an exceptionally rich collection of Italian Renaissance and Baroque painting, which was later enlarged by the selection of exquisite Italian primitives donated by Bishop Arnold Ipolyi. Károly Pulszky's deliberate purchases in Italy, together with the Pálffy Collection and some recent acquisitions to fill still existing gaps, have raised the Italian section of the Gallery to a point where it can be favourably compared with collections found in other countries. Here the history of Italian painting can be traced from the thirteenth century to the late eighteenth century in major works representing almost every school and trend, including a number of masterpieces renowned throughout the world.

The wide-ranging selection of German and Austrian paintings can again be traced to historic links and individual enterprise in the past. A considerable number of German and Austrian painters chose to work in Hungary or accepted commissions from Hungarians, while Austria was easily accessible to collectors. The Pyrker and the Esterházy collections included relatively few, though exquisite, paintings from this region. Masterpieces by Dürer and Cranach came to the Museum with the items transferred from the Buda Castle. Most of the fifteenth- and sixteenth-century panels originated from Bishop Ipolyi's collection, while the particularly rich collection of eighteenth-century paintings were acquired with the Zichy Collection. Recently, a chronological gap in this section has been filled, by purchase or donation of a number of German works from the seventeenth century.

During the nineteenth century Hungarian collectors were attracted to Netherlandish paintings because of their clearly intelligible secular themes, small size, and the fact that they were readily available at modest prices. Relatively few examples of early Netherlandish painting have reached Budapest, but seventeenth- and Dutch painting is well represented and includes splendid works in a rich variety of genres. Some of these paintings, masterpieces by Rubens, Rembrandt, Van Dyck and Franz Hals, came to the Museum as part of the Esterházy Collection, and more Netherlandish works came into the Museum's possession between 1951 and 1953 with the acquisition of the Zichy and the György Ráth collections. The Netherlandish section, which is still enriched with new acquisitions, now comprises a comprehensive and valuable collection containing not only works of great artistic value but also an extensive range of relatively rare pictures by minor Dutch masters.

The most important collection in the Museum, the one most frequently appraised, is the collection of Spanish paintings. Beyond the borders of Spain there is scarcely any museum in Europe which can display such a complete illustration of the development of Spanish painting. The collection comprises about seventy works and includes a number of masterpieces. There are seven works by El Greco, one by Ribera, three by Murillo, three by Zurbarán, one by Velázquez and five by Goya. There are also representative works of lesser known but important painters, who had some influence on the development of Spanish art (for instance Luis Tristán, Alonso Cano, Eugenio Caxes, Francisco de Herrera and Juan Antonio Escalante). For this superb collection the Museum is indebted first of all to the collecting zeal of the Esterházy family, and secondly to the skill with which the Budapest collector Marcell Nemes acquired works in Spain. It was Prince Pál Esterházy who became interested in the collection made by Edmund Bourke in London; he who persuaded his family to buy twenty-two of Bourke's paintings in 1819. They bought another twenty-six from Bourke's widow at a later date, most of them works by Spanish masters. When the pictures arrived at the Esterházy Gallery, Josef Fischer, the curator, rightly commented that the Prince had acquired works by an interesting and completely new school of masters "who are as yet unknown here". The Goya pictures purchased at the auction of the Kaunitz Collection in Vienna further enriched the Spanish Collection, which, from the Esterházy treasures of the National Picture Gallery eventually entered the Museum of Fine Arts, where the Spanish collection was further enlarged by state acquisitions and by the contribution of Marcell Nemes, an early admirer of El Greco's art. Around the turn of the last century he acquired a great many paintings by this Spanish artist, and six of them have found their way to the Museum. In 1922 and 1930, valuable works were donated to the Museum for the Spanish collection by Colonel Jenő Boross.

In November, 1983, a disturbing event shook the life of the Museum. Hungarian and Italian criminals broke into the Gallery of Old Masters and ran off with seven extremely valuable paintings (Raphael's *Portrait of Pietro Bembo* and *Esterházy Madonna,* Giorgione's *Self-portrait,* Tintoretto's *Portrait of a Woman* and *Portrait of a Man,* G. D. Tiepolo's *The Resting on the Flight into Egypt* and G. B. Tiepolo's *The Virgin with Six Saints*). However, as a result of the cuccessful endeavours of the authorities, these masterpieces were soon back in their places.

In the Gallery of Old Masters there are around 2,500 paintings. More than 600 works are on permanent display in 23 rooms and 17 cabinets on the first floor. These outstanding, representative works provide an almost totally comprehensive record of the development of European painting from the thirteenth century to the eighteenth century arranged in chronological order but with due regard to the historical, stylistic and geographic connections of the works.

The Italian section begins with altarpieces by thirteenth-century Tuscan masters, Florentine and Sienese painters of the fourteenth and fifteenth centuries, and it illustrates the development of late Gothic and early Renaissance painting with works by Spinello Aretino, Sassetta, Domenico Ghirlandaio, Francesco Francia and others. The Italian Renaissance is represented by a succession of masterpieces. Giorgio-

ne's *Portrait of a Man,* Raphael's *Portrait of Pietro Bembo* and his *Esterházy Madonna,* two Madonnas by Boltraffio, *The Virgin and Child with an Angel (Madonna del Latte)* by Correggio, Piombo's *Portrait of a Man* and *Christ Bearing the Cross,* and works by Titian, Tintoretto, Veronese, Lorenzo Lotto and Palma Vecchio are all superb examples of this decisive phase in the history of European art. Limited space and the size of most Italian Mannerist and Baroque paintings restrict the number of works on display. Nevertheless, works by Annibale Carracci, Guercino, Francesco Furini, Domenico Fetti, Bernardo Strozzi and Guido Reni give a very good idea of the principal stylistic endeavours of the time. Works by Sebastiano Ricci, Giovanni Battista Tiepolo, Francesco Solimena and Francesco Guardi, partly recent purchases, indicate the range of artistic endeavour in the eighteenth century in Italy.

Leaving the Italian collection we come to the area which houses the Netherlandish Collection which includes Petrus Christus's *Virgin and Child,* Gerard David's *Nativity,* Memling's *Calvary Triptych,* and the world-famous *St. John the Baptist Preaching* by Pieter Bruegel the Elder, the portrait *Emperor Charles V* by Barend van Orley, and *Market Scene,* by Pieter Aersten. Flemish painting of the seventeenth century is represented by Rubens, Van Dyck and Jordaens, and there are typical landscapes, genre pieces and still-lifes by Adriaen Brouwer, David Teniers the Younger, Frans Snyders and others.

Of the seventeenth-century Dutch paintings displayed in two rooms and nine cabinets the most outstanding are Rembrandt's *The Dream of St. Joseph, The Old Rabbi* and *The Slaughtered Ox,* Willem Buytewech's *A Merry Company* and two portraits by Frans Hals. There are also valuable works by Rembrandt's pupils and followers such as Nicholas Maes, Aert de Gelder, and Gerbrandt van den Eeckhout. Only a few of the numerous Dutch genre paintings, portraits, landscapes and still-lifes owned by the Museum can be put on permanent view. The finest pieces are the pictures of Salomon and Jacob van Ruisdael, Jan van Goyen, Jan Vermeer van Delft, Pieter de Hooch and Adriaen van Ostade.

The French section houses a relatively modest collection which

Visitors viewing the Spanish paintings in the Gallery of Old Masters

nevertheless illustrates the varied themes and choice of styles adopted by seventeenth-century masters such as Nicolas Poussin, Claude Lorrain, Simon Vouet, Pierre Mignard, and Nicolas de Largillière. Eighteenth-century French art, however, is represented only by a few works by Jean-Baptiste Siméon Chardin, Hubert Robert, Louis-Léopold Boilly and Jean-Baptiste Greuze. The Spanish collection is justifiably famous and is suitably exhibited in four large galleries. An interesting feature here is the abundance of fifteenth- and sixteenth-century works, rarely encountered outside Spain. Equally remarkable are the seven El Grecos, including *Mary Magdalene, The Agony in the Garden*, and the dramatic and visionary *Annunciation*. The art of Ribera, who worked in Naples, is represented by his monumental *Martyrdom of St. Andrew*. There is also a Velázquez, an early genre painting from Seville, *Peasants at Table*. Murillo and Zurbarán are each represented by three important works. Goya's pictures in the Museum—*The Water Seller (La aguadora), The Knife-grinder (El afilador)* and the *Portrait of the Wife of Juan Agostin Céan Bermúdez*—are among the most popular and highly regarded works in the history of European painting. In addition to these masterpieces the collection includes twenty major works by other Spanish masters.

Early German and Austrian painting is well illustrated by works dating back to the fifteenth century. These, together with works from the sixteenth, seventeenth and eighteenth centuries are housed in four galleries and a cabinet. Among the early works a worthy place is assigned to the panel by Hans Holbein the Elder depicting *The Death of the Virgin* and the polyptych of the *Strigel Altar*. German Renaissance is represented by numerous works, among them Dürer's *Portrait of a Man*, three important works by Albrecht Altdorfer representing the Danube School, and several fine paintings by Hans Baldung Grien, Jörg Breu and Lucas Cranach the Elder. Seventeenth-century German painting features in an interesting selection of works by Johann Heinrich Schönfeld, Christoph Paudiss, Nicolaus Knüpfer and Johann König, while the eighteenth century is introduced by a rich choice of altarpieces, sketches for ceilings, portraits and landscapes by leading masters of

the various schools—Johann Kupetzky, Daniel Gran, Franz Anton Maulbertsch, Angelica Kauffmann, Anton Raphael Mengs and others.

English painting cannot be properly studied in the European museums outside the British Isles. This lends particular importance to the collection in Budapest. The Museum collection includes works by Thomas Gainsborough, William Hogarth, Joshua Reynolds, Henry Raeburn and Thomas Lawrence, thus illustrating the development of eighteenth-century British portraiture, while landscape painting is represented by a few attractive Constables.

European Sculpture

In the Museum of Fine Arts the Department of Sculpture was established as a result of the efforts made by Károly Pulszky. As a curator of the National Picture Gallery he visited Italy in 1894–95, where he bought valuable paintings and 121 sculptures. These were mainly Italian, some of them decorative stone carvings, and some exquisite works such as *The Archangel Gabriel* by Agostino di Duccio and a *Madonna* by Michelozzo Michelozzi. From these modest beginnings the collection gained new status when, in 1914, the Museum purchased a collection owned by the heirs of the great Hungarian master of neo-Classicism, István Ferenczy. His collection, which had sunk into undeserved oblivion, enriched the Museum with works of exceptional value. It consisted mainly of bronze statues, and included the *Putto with Dolphin* from Verrocchio's workshop, *The Rape of Europa* by Andrea Riccio, *Heracles* by Alessandro Algardi, and the world-famous small equestrian bronze linked with the name of Leonardo da Vinci and considered to be the work of the master.

Two fine reliefs in lead by Georg Raphael Donner, the eighteenth-century Austrian sculptor, have also come from the Ferenczy Collection. Well considered purchases and felicitous donations further enlarged the collection with Italian Renaissance and fifteenth to seventeenth century German works, so that the Museum catalogue for 1921 could claim that "not only have we commenced to develop a collection of sculpture in a universal direction, but have also laid its

foundations for a more fortunate future". The enlarged collection was gradually classified with the result that some of the sculptures in the Historical Museum and the Museum of Applied Arts were transferred to the Museum of Fine Arts. It acquired sculptures also from the Budapest Zichy Gallery and the György Ráth Museum in the 1950s.

More recently the collection has been almost doubled in size and has gained an international reputation as a comprehensive collection of valuable works representing a variety of styles and many periods.

European sculpture spanning a period of around ten centuries is exhibited in a number of galleries on each floor of the building. In the so-called "Renaissance Hall" on the ground floor there is a selection of Venetian fountains while a selection of decorative carvings can be seen on the staircase. In the galleries of the second floor the development of Italian sculpture can be traced back from the Middle Ages to the seventeenth century: besides the famous works mentioned above, there is a large collection of sculptures, as varied in material as in theme, by Andrea Pisano, Luca della Robbia, Benedetto da Maiano, Jacopo Sansovino and Alessandro Vittoria. The next gallery and the mezzanine between the first and second storeys contain a fine selection of fourteenth- to seventeenth-century German and Austrian statues, medieval carvings, exquisite wooden statues by the circles of Multscher and Riemenschneider and sculptures and reliefs by Hans Leinberger, Leonhard Kern, Johann Meinrad Guggenbichler, Georg Raphael Donner and Franz Xaver Messerschmidt. Despite some major recent acquisitions, the collection of French, Netherlandish and Spanish sculpture is less extensive. Some of the mediaeval, seventeenth- and eighteenth-century sculptures are of the highest quality, for instance the bronze by Adriaen de Vries, the figures of saints from Michel Colombe's workshop and the *Amor* of Jean-Baptiste Pigalle.

Prints and Drawings

The Department has a collection of around 10,000 drawings and 100,000 engravings, but they are too sensitive to light and thus cannot be put on permanent display. Temporary exhibitions are

therefore arranged in the ground floor gallery, where selections of drawings, engravings or etchings are chosen to illustrate some particular theme, technique or the work of a particular artist.

Many of the works, including the superb Italian Renaissance and Baroque drawings, were part of the Esterházy collection purchased by the state in 1870.

Among the most famous of these treasures are Leonardo da Vinci's red and black chalk drawings of *Warrior's heads,* and sketches by Raphael, Correggio, Veronese, Guercino, and the Tiepolos. The greater part of the collection was purchased in the early nineteenth century, one of the major acquisitions of that period being Cavaliere Poggi's famous Paris collection of drawings. The majority of the equally rich selection of Netherlandish drawings came from the Nowohratsky-Kollowrath Collection in Prague. They were bought by the Esterházy family in 1803, and they included 15 drawings by Rembrandt, significant works by Rubens, Van Dyck and Jordaens and also works by some minor masters.

German art is represented by a number of studies by Dürer, Altdorfer, Wolf Huber and Lucas Cranach the Elder, some of these works originating from the notable Praun Collection amassed during the seventeenth and eighteenth centuries in Nürnberg. French works from the Esterházy Collection include valuable seventeenth- and eighteenth-century drawings by Poussin, Watteau, Fragonard and others.

The Esterházy Collection of drawings totalled 3,535 sheets, and has been further enlarged by later bequests, donations and purchases. In 1901, for instance, István Delhaes, a Hungarian painter and collector, who died in Vienna, bequeathed some fine studies and sketches by Troger and Maulbertsch to the Museum, thus filling a gap among the works of eighteenth-century German and Austrian masters. The Delhaes bequest comprised 2,683 drawings which provided a starting-point for the collection of nineteenth-century drawings representing the Biedermeier style, neo-Classicism and Romanticism. The collection of nineteenth-century and modern drawings was greatly enhanced in 1934 by the acquisition of a collection made by Pál Majovszky, an eminent Budapest art patron. His collection included works of exceptional beauty and value such as the watercolour *Horse Frightened by Lightning* by Delacroix, *Barricade* and *Rue de Berne in Rain* by Manet, and a number of sketches by Renoir, Cézanne, Degas, Rodin, Daumier and Toulouse-Lautrec. Regular purchases and individual donations have further augmented the collection of drawings in recent decades, particularly in the field of twentieth-century masters. Significant donations (for instance by Fritz Kahnweiler and Victor Vasarely) and purchases have enriched the collection with works by the leading masters of the period such as Picasso, Chagall, Kokoschka, Rodchenko and Vasarely. The work of younger artists has also been given space in the Museum: we can see the latest trends of many countries. These are exhibited in a succession of temporary exhibitions arranged in the Department of Modern Art, together with paintings, sculptures and mobiles.

The prints, of which the Museum owns around 100,000, are kept in portfolios though selections of them are regularly on view in temporary exhibitions. About 50,000 of the prints originate from the Esterházy collection. The collection illustrates the development of European graphic art from the beginning of the fifteenth century to the present day, and includes examples of practically every type of graphic art—print, woodcuts, engravings, etchings, mezzotints, lithographs and seriographs.

The Department owns series of prints, in each case almost complete, made by the most eminent artists of the medium: Dürer, Lucas van Leyden, Callot, Rembrandt, Goya and Daumier.

The Department of Prints and Drawings is well known for its scholarly publications and its educational activities. Some of the treasures in the Department have been exhibited abroad (in Vienna, Prague, Leningrad and Bordeaux), and some have been included in several great international exhibitions. In Hungary temporary exhibitions are always popular and exhibition catalogues with scholarly notes are also published in Hungarian and in foreign languages when such exhibitions are arranged.

Modern Art

The Gallery of Old Masters on the first floor leads directly into the gallery housing the collection of the Department of Modern Art. This relatively new collection is neither as valuable nor as comprehensive as the collection of Old Masters.

Originally the collection was divided between the National Museum and the National Picture Gallery, and comprised mainly nineteenth-century Austrian Biedermeier paintings. In 1912 the Pálffy Collection was bequeathed to the Museum, which included pictures by Franz von Lenbach, Charles-François Daubigny and Constantin Troyon. Thus it meant a very modest increase in the number of French and German paintings. However, from 1910 onwards single paintings were bought, donations accepted, and the collection increased. Monet's *Apple-trees in Blossom* was purchased in Berlin in 1912, while Gauguin's masterpiece, *Black Pigs* and Toulouse-Lautrec's enchanting *Ces Dames* were bought at an exhibition at the Ernst Museum in 1913. The following years saw the acquisition of Manet's famous *Lady with Fan,* and the eminent Budapest collector Ferenc Hatvany donated important works by Pissarro and Cézanne. The years between the two world wars showed growing interest in contemporary endeavours including the latest French trends, which led to the acquisition of paintings by Bonnard, Utrillo and others. Since 1945, the Museum has adopted a deliberate policy of building up the collection of nineteenth- and twentieth-century works. In 1945–46 some fine works by Corot, Monet and Renoir were purchased from the former Herzog Collection, and in 1951 one of Gustave Courbet's most famous paintings, *The Wrestlers,* was bought from the Hatvany Collection. Recently the Museum has acquired paintings by Max Slevogt, Oskar Kokoschka and Marc Chagall.

The range of contemporary art has been rapidly extended. This project has been greatly facilitated by donations from eminent artists of Hungarian extraction living abroad, as well as the stimulus of exhibitions of foreign art arranged in Hungary. As a result of the above-mentioned development, the nucleus of the paintings in the Modern Art Collection has remained to this day the selection of nineteenth-century German and Austrian paintings, the French paintings representing the period from Romanticism to Post-Impressionism, and the interesting and varied work of certain contemporary artists.

Limited space on the first floor permits the permanent exhibition of only the very finest paintings. The Austrian Biedermeier artists are represented by the work of Ferdinand Georg Waldmüller, Franz Eybl and Friedrich von Amerling, and nineteenth-century German painting is represented by the works of Franz von Lenbach, Wilhelm Leibl, Arnold Böcklin and Adolf von Menzel. Paintings by the landscapists of the Barbizon School, which played a significant part in the development of Hungarian painting, and works by the great Romantics, Eugène Delacroix and Théodore Chassériau, are grouped beside some of the paintings of Camille Corot and Gustave Courbet, Pierre Puvis de Chavannes, Eugène Carrière and Maurice Denis.

Certain outstanding works by the French Impressionists are worthy of special mention, for instance the paintings by Édouard Manet, Claude Monet, Camille Pissarro and Auguste Renoir. The artists of the succeeding generation are also well represented, the variety of their endeavours illustrated in paintings by Paul Gauguin, Henri de Toulouse-Lautrec, Paul Cézanne, Maurice Utrillo and André Lhote. The art of other European countries—nineteenth-century Italian, Belgian, Dutch, Swedish, Polish, Swiss and Finnish art—is represented only by a random selection of paintings which can only hint at the range and variety of their national endeavours.

A large gallery on the ground floor houses the nineteenth-century sculptures included in the collection of Modern Art. However, just like the paintings, they cannot provide a totally comprehensive view of the period. Because of historical connections, it is only natural that most of the acquisitions should be Austrian and German. However, during the early years of the twentieth century immense interest was shown in Auguste Rodin's innovative sculptures and the singular work of the Belgian Constantin Meunier, both of whom are represented by a number of works. The collection of French and Belgian sculpture has also been considerably enlarged by the works of Jean-Baptiste Carpeaux, Charles Despiau, Aristide Joseph Maillol and George Minne. The difficulties inherent in the acquisition of large works partly account for the limitations of the collection, which provides only a fragmentary idea of the stylistic trends and genres of nineteenth-century European sculpture. On the other hand, it is particularly attractive because it contains masterpieces by the Danish artist Bertel Thorvaldsen, the Russian sculptor, Pavel Petrovich Trubetzkoy, Ivan Meštrović from Yugoslavia, Medardo Rosso from Italy and Fritz Cramer from Germany.

In accordance with recent artistic endeavours, contemporary sculptures are shown together with paintings and graphic works in the ground-floor galleries assigned to display twentieth-century art.

The works exhibited are changed whenever new acquisitions are made. One can see here a selection of fine paintings by Oskar Kokoschka, Marc Chagall, Pablo Picasso, Victor Vasarely, Kurt Schwitters, Renato Guttuso and others, together with sculptures and mobiles by Emilio Greco, Fritz Wotruba, Étienne Hajdu, Pierre Székely, Amerigo Tot and Nicolas Schöffer.

General Information

Directors of the Museum of Fine Arts:
1906–1914 Ernő Kammerer
1914–1935 Elek Petrovics
1935–1944 Dénes Csánky
1945–1949 István Genthon
1949–1952 Imre Oltványi
1952–1955 Ferenc Redő
1956–1964 Andor Pigler
1964–1984 Klára Garas
1984–   Ferenc Merényi

Museum Publications:
J. PEREGRINY:
Az Országos Magyar Szépművészeti Múzeum állagai (Catalogue of the Hungarian National Museum of Fine Arts). Budapest, 1909–1915
G. TÉREY:
Országos Magyar Szépművészeti Múzeum. A régi képtár teljes leíró lajstroma I. (The Hungarian National Museum of Fine Arts. A Complete Descriptive Catalogue of the Gallery of Old Masters). Berlin, 1916 (Hungarian and German editions)
G. TÉREY:
Az Országos Magyar Szépművészeti Múzeum Régi Képtárának katalógusa (Catalogue of the Gallery of Old Masters in the Hungarian National Museum of Fine Arts). Budapest, 1924 (Hungarian and English editions)

A. HEKLER:
Die Antiken in Budapest, Erste Abteilung: Die Skulpturen. Vienna, 1929
Z. OROSZLÁN:
Az Országos Szépművészeti Múzeum antik terrakottagyűjteményének katalógusa (Catalogue of the Collection of Terracotta Antiquities in the National Museum of Fine Arts). Budapest, 1930
A. PIGLER:
A Régi Képtár katalógusa (Catalogue of the Gallery of Old Masters). Budapest, 1937 and 1954
A. PIGLER:
Katalog der Galerie Alter Meister. Budapest, 1967
A Szépművészeti Múzeum 1906–1956 (The Museum of Fine Arts, 1906–1956). Budapest, 1956
T. SZENTLÉLEKY:
Ancient Lamps. Budapest, 1969
K. GARAS:
Paintings in the Museum of Fine Arts. Budapest, 1973 (also in

Restorer at work

Hungarian, German, French, Polish, Czech and Russian)
J. BALOGH:
Katalog der ausländischen Bildwerke des Museums der Bildenden Künste in Budapest. Budapest, 1975
T. GERSZI:
A németalföldi rajzművészet két évszázada (Two Centuries of Netherlandish Drawing). Budapest, 1976 (also in German, Dutch and French)
K. GARAS:
XVIII. sz. német és osztrák rajzok (Eighteenth-century German and Austrian Drawings). Budapest, 1980 (also in German)
J. GY. SZILÁGYI:
Corpus Vasorum Antiquorum. Hongrie I, Budapest 1981

The Character of the Collections:
The collections include works of international art ranging from ancient times to the present day. There are six departments: Egyptian Art (3,530 items); Classical Antiquities (4,400 items); Sculpture (343 items); Old Masters

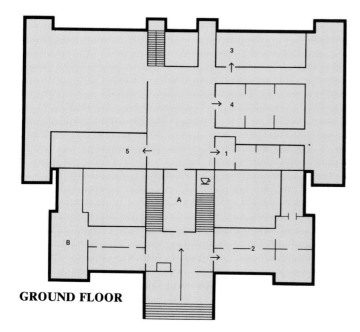

GROUND FLOOR

1. Egyptian Art
2. Classical Antiquities
3. Prints and Drawings
4. Modern Sculpture
5. Modern Art
A. The Marble Hall ⎫ temporary
B. The Pergamon Hall ⎰ exhibitions

Floor plans for the collections of the Museum of Fine Arts

1ST FLOOR

Old Masters: galleries I–XXIII and cabinets 1–18
Modern Art A–B and C–H

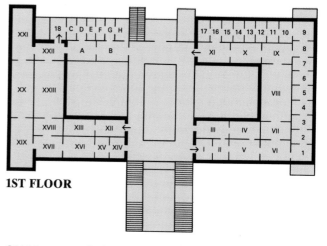

Old Sculpture

1+1/2 FLOORS

2ND FLOOR

15

(2,500 items); Modern Art (19th and 20th-century works, 900 items) and Prints and Drawings (approximately 10,000 drawings and 100,000 prints).

The Director, responsible for the administration of the Museum, is assisted by the curators of the six Departments.

The Reference Library contains approximately 80,000 volumes on the history of the arts and it is open to scholars, students and the public on weekdays.

The restoration of paintings, sculptures and other objects is undertaken in the Museum workshop. There is also a photographic laboratory.

Lighting: Some of the galleries have glass roofing. In all of the building there is also artificial illumination.

Visitors: Since 1982 visitors to the Museum have numbered around 380,000, yearly.

Opening hours: From Tuesday to Sunday the Museum is open from 10 a.m. to 6 p.m. It is closed on Mondays and national holidays. Entrance fee: five forints for adults, with reduced fees or free admittance for students, groups and senior citizens. Admission is free on Saturdays. The reserve collections can be visited by scholars and students by appointment.

Lectures: There are regular guided tours in each department, with special exhibitions and lectures on Sundays. There are also classes for children, clubs for young people, senior citizens, and study circles.

Egyptian Art

1. *Grave relief*: fragment

1. *Relief,* painted limestone (fragment, 15.2×9.7 cm), part of a series of reliefs covering the inner wall of a mastaba from the Old Kingdom. The portrait of a bearded man with a white *sash* over one shoulder could very well be part of a scene depicting a funeral procession. The man's beard, a symbol of dignity, the hair falling to his shoulders and his attire indicate that he may have been one of the priests in the procession. The depth of the relief is scarcely 3–4 mm, and the surface is carefully painted. The style of the portrait and the artistic standard of the work seem to indicate that the fragment dates back to the period of the Fifth Dynasty and comes from Saqqara.

2. *Portrait of a Nobleman,* limestone (22 cm in height), originally part of a seated or kneeling figure from a tomb as borne out by the upper edge of the back support set in the lower edge of the wig at the back of the neck. It is a portrait of a young nobleman, his rank is indicated by the short ornate beard, the ears pierced for pendants, and above all by the richly curled wig. The latter is meticulously carved and provides a perfectly proportioned frame for the head. The features are refined and ageless, recalling the style of the Theban sculpture of the Ramesside period. The downward tapering lines of the slender neck draw attention to the beautifully poised head, which reinforces the significance of the funerary statue—apotheosis in the afterworld. By analogy and stylistic marks, the head would appear to be the work of a Theban sculptor of the Nineteenth Dynasty of the New Kingdom.

2. *Portrait of a Nobleman*

17

3. *Funerary papyrus*

3. The third and last section of a painted *funerary papyrus* (total length 100 cm), belonging to the group known as the mythological papyri, which were prepared for the Theban priests of the god Amon at the time of the Theban theocracy. The series of pictures with their complicated contents represent ideas related to the Sun's voyage through the underworld, demons and the destiny of the deceased. This papyrus depicts gods of the underworld. The order of the scenes is from right to left. Mummy-shaped deities are depicted within the curves of the huge serpent and the disc of the Sun rising between the double serpent can be recognized as an allegorical representation of the forces capable of influencing the fate of the dead.

The soul (or *ba*) of the deceased, shown in the form of a bird with a man's head, prays beside a small offering table, in front of a serpent-headed barque set upon the symbol of the sky, with the disc of the rising Sun over it, with the magic eye of the Sun God inside.

The next scene, with the two scarabs and the figure of the green-faced mummy of Osiris signifying revival, marks the end of the Sun's voyage. The red disc of the rising sun is seen above the semicircular horizon, between the outstretched arms of the god of the air. The sunrise was also thought to influence the destiny of the deceased, who rises together with the sun and travels with it across the sky. The missing section of the papyrus would have included the name of the deceased, a Theban priest of Amon during the Twenty-first Dynasty (Third Intermediate Period).

4. A bronze statuette of *Imhotep*, renowned architect of the Third Dynasty, later a legendary figure venerated as the patron of learning and sciences. In the Saite Period he was deified. His wisdom is here symbolized by the open papyrus roll held across his knees. From the Saite Period onwards he continued to be immortalized in votive bronze statues, which were placed in and around his sanctuary (supposed to have been somewhere near Memphis). This bronze statuette (height: 22 cm) is one of the most artistically executed relics in the collection. Imhotep is shown seated on a throne with open-work ornamentation and a pedestal. His close fitting head-dress resembles that worn by the god Ptah. Around his neck he wears a wide rounded collar embellished with gold inlay and engraving. His close-fitting, ankle-length robe, tied under the chest, reveals the splendid proportions of the construction as a whole. The open papyrus roll on his knees bears an inscription and an architectural design. His feet rest on a small pedestal with votive inscriptions on all four sides. The statue was made by the process known as *cire perdue* or lost wax: after careful casting the different parts were fitted together, then embellished with engravings and inlaid work and finally, polished.
The statuette is thought to date from the first half of the Ptolemaic Period. Like the majority of the Imhotep bronzes, it probably comes from Memphis.

4. *Statuette of Imhotep enthroned*

5. A painted wooden *funerary stele* (49.3×31.5 cm) is dominated by the winged disc of the sun placed in the centre of the curved upper hand. Below the sun there is a scarab with a sitting jackal on either side and two of crowned uraeus snakes' heads and short inscriptions. The accentuated pictorial band depicts (from right to left) a deceased woman in festive array as she is led by the jackal-headed Anubis before the enthroned god Osiris, ruler of the underworld. The inscription tells us that the woman is called Tamerti. She holds her heart or a vase containing a burning offering in her left hand. Behind the throne of Osiris stand the falcon-headed god Horus and his divine mother Isis. The lower part of the funerary stele contains ten lines of horizontal hieroglyphic inscription, expounding a royal order of Osiris in which he calls upon the deities and the cosmic gods of Amon-Re, Atum, Ptah and Nun, to witness the apotheosis of the deceased woman. Tamerti, the subject of the stele, was a musician of the Theban god Amon-Re with the rank of a priestess, and her parents also had been members of the priesthood of Amon. The stele itself comes from the Theban necropolis and dates from about the fourth century B.C. These wooden grave tablets were originally fitted into stepped pedestals, missing.

5. *Grave tablet*

Classical Antiquities

1. *Couple lying on a bed*

2. *Athenian black-figure amphora.* This vase, 37.6 cm in height, was acquired in the 1860s in Italy by a Hungarian collector. According to Greek myth, Metis, the personification of wise counsel, was swallowed by Zeus to prevent the birth of her child. Afterwards, Pallas Athene sprang, fully-armed, from a breach in Zeus' skull which Hephaestus made with his hammer. On one side of the vase Zeus is shown at the moment before the birth, centrally placed and seated, attended on either side by the Eileithyiai, the goddesses who aided women in childbirth. This was a favourite subject of sixth-century B.C. Athenian vase painting. The Budapest vase was also painted by an Athenian master around 540–530 B.C., using the technique of black-figure painting. On one of his vases the painter depicted a swinging girl, therefore he was named the "Swing Painter". More than 150 vases painted by him are known, an indication of the persistence with which he sought new solutions both in his mythological scenes and those taken from everyday life. On the other side of the vase there are figures of young men racing.

1. *Couple lying on a bed.* Length: 10.2 cm, terracotta, hand-shaped. This statuette is a rare example of the terracotta statuettes typical of the late phase of Mycenaean culture in the fourteenth and thirteenth centuries B.C. Like other vases of the period, they were painted before firing. This style of sculpture, presumed to be of Cretan origin and possibly influenced by Near Eastern cultures, is characterized by the virtual reduction of human figures into symbols. Most of the statuettes depict standing female figures and so far no other piece similar to the Budapest one has been found. A close relationship between the two figures is indicated by the position of the arm of the figure on the left and by the fact that the figures are lightly turned to face each other. The figures could represent a ritual marriage or lovers alive or dead, i.e. the statuette could have religious or profane significance, depending on where it was found—in a sanctuary, a house or a grave. The bed appears to have consisted of rush matting over a low wooden structure resting on four feet, and the wavy lines may indicate a coverlet. The statuette is one of the earliest group compositions of Greek art, early prototypes of which are known from Mesopotamia.

3. *Athenian red-figure kylix.* This is the most valuable vase in the collection, purchased in the 1850s by a Hungarian painter in Rome. The cup, 21.4 cm in diameter, comes from the workshop of the potter Andokides. The painter, usually called the Andokides Painter after the owner of the workshop, was a pupil of Exekias, the greatest master of black-figure vase painting, and in all probability he was the first to employ the red-figure technique. The Budapest cup exhibits black-figure traditions both in its shape and ornamentation, but the male figure on one side of the cup and the hurrying woman on the other, between the apotropaic eyes—potent against malign powers—which virtually animate the kylix, are the late work of the Andokides Painter from the years around 520 B.C. This is the only surviving red-figure cup by the painter, who favoured the ornamentation of large amphorae. The drinking figure probably represents Heracles, the favourite protagonist of the painter's mythological scenes. His art must have been held in high esteem primarily by the Etruscans, for none of his 16 red-figure vases discovered so far have been found in Greece.

2. *Athenian black-figure amphora*

3. *Athenian red-figure kylix*

21

4. *The Grimani Jug.* This was one of the Greek treasures acquired by the Venetian Grimani family in Athens in the sixteenth century. It was bought from an art dealer in Venice in 1833 by Ferenc Pulszky, who later became director of the Hungarian National Museum. This Greek bronze of the highest quality (31.2 cm in height) originates, together with some other items of related style and ornamentation, from a Peloponnesian workshop, probably in Corinth. The figure of a siren can be seen at the base of the separately cast handle, which is fitted to the body of the jug hammered from a bronze plate. This was a favourite motif in the decoration of Greek bronze vessels, while the figure of Silenus above the mouthpiece, with a drinking horn held in both hands, is a motif applied less frequently. Both the style of the figures and the shape of the jug indicate a date of around 460–450 B.C., the years of transition between the early Classical and the high Classical periods.

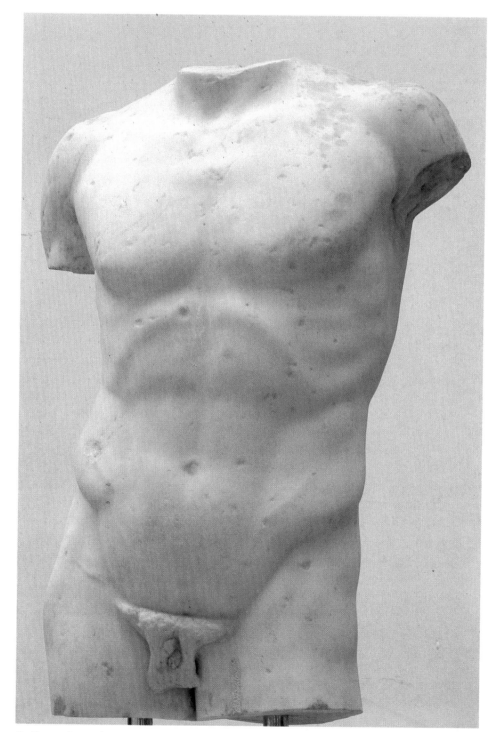

5. *Torso of a youth*

5. *Torso of a Youth.* This marble statue, 76.4 cm high, was in the Cappelli Collection in Florence in the nineteenth century and it was only recently acquired by the Museum from a Hungarian private collection. In the last century the torso was completed to portray a Roman commander, but since the removal of the modern additions it is possible to see more clearly the reference to the Greek original, the *Doryphorus* (lance-bearer) made around 440 B.C. by Polyclitus who, with Pheidias, is counted among the greatest sculptors of the Greek Classical period. In one of his writings Polyclitus himself formulated the basic laws for representing the human body as based on his *Doryphoros*, which exhibits the classical method for achieving balance and proportion so well. Traditionally the statue was thought to represent Achilles. It became the model for many works of Greek art in the decades following its origin, was unanimously praised by contemporary authors and its influence was still felt in the period of the Roman Empire. The delicate copy now in Budapest presumably dates from the reign of Trajan or Hadrian and is said to have been found in Pompeii.

6. *Head of Minerva,* terracotta, life-size, helmeted, with shoulder-length hair. This is a fragment of a full-length statue. According to written sources, inscriptions and representations, the goddess was worshipped by the non-Greek population of Italy at least from the sixth century B.C. onwards. Her attributes, including the helmet, were taken over from the Greek Athena, and she was worshipped by the Latins, Etruscans and other Italian peoples under the name of Minerva. The terracotta head in Budapest is a fragment of one of the earliest known large sculptures of the goddess in Italy; it was either made for a sanctuary like the statues recently found in Lavinium or it may have decorated the roof of a temple. The features indicate that it was made in a southern Etruscan workshop around 470 B.C. Marble was still practically unknown at the time in Italy and terracotta was often used for monumental sculpture.

6. *Minerva head*

7. *Athenian stele with three figures*

7. *Athenian stele with three figures.* This high relief sculpture, 168 cm high, was purchased by the Museum in 1928. It dates from the last phase of the art of Attic Classical funerary sculpture, around 330–320 B.C. During the fourth century B.C. the scenes on Greek stelae bear witness to a new development in the concept of human values. The group compositions emphasize firm family ties that outlast individual mortality, a concept expressed with hitherto unknown pathos. Towards the end of the Classical age it had become customary to give the deceased the heroic features which would indicate how far removed he now was from the living. The aged male figure in this relief is set apart from human existence by his nakedness, and his inward glance indicates that his feelings are very different from those of the female figure standing next to him. The master of the stele is called the "Budapest Sculptor", in tribute to this highly individualistic work of late classical art in Athens.

8. *Niobid,* terracotta, 67 cm high. Proud of her seven sons and seven daughters, Niobe belittled Leto, whose children, Apollo and Artemis, avenged the insult to their mother by killing all her children, the Niobids. The myth was popular among Hellenistic sculptors as it was especially suited to exploit the newly discovered possibilities inherent in three-dimensional composition. The statue depicting one of the Niobids originates from the S. Maria Capua Vetere, and was probably one of a group of statues adorning the pediment of a temple. The youth, a type also found in late Hellenistic Greek sculpture, is shown trying to protect himself from the deadly arrows of the divine pair by drawing his robe over his head. This late masterpiece of Italian terracotta statuary blends the traditions of the Etruscan culture of Capua with forms of Hellenistic art in Asia Minor, transmitted from southern Italy.

8. *Niobid*

9. *Bust of a Man.* Marble, 55 cm high. The bust is somewhat larger than life-size, the serene, meditative features suggesting an outstanding figure in the intellectual life of the day. A similar impression is created by another portrait of the same man in the Thessaloniki Museum. The beard and hair-style recall the portraits of Greek philosophers and poets of the Classical period but the slight turn of the head and the look in the eyes reveal a psychological approach unknown in Classical Antiquity. The duality in which a nostalgic imitation of Classical models is mingled with features pointing to the realities of the present, is typical of the period and provenance of the portrait—possibly the last quarter of the second century A.D. in a Greek town in Asia Minor. This part of Roman-occupied Greece experienced a new golden age in the second century, particularly from the reign of Hadrian onwards. This was also promoted by the mixture of esteem and contempt felt by the Romans for Hellenism; in such a climate literary and artistic works were appreciated mainly through the depressing realization that the intellectual excitement of a previous age was no longer in evidence.

10. *Roman relief,* marble fragment in two sections, total length: 122 cm. The principal figure of the right section, and obviously of the relief as a whole, is the god Apollo shown seated on a rock and holding a *kithara* in his hand, behind him there is a three-legged cauldron referring to the Delphic Oracle, and in front of him there are parts of boats. The three men on the left are part of a ceremonial procession, the one in the middle being a musician blowing a tuba. The two fragments are from one continuous relief, but it is not certain that they are reproduced here in the original order. Nevertheless the subject is not in doubt: the relief commemorates the decisive naval victory of Augustus over the fleets of Mark Anthony near the promontory of Actium (in modern north-western Greece) in 31 B.C., a victory which the emperor attributed to the supporting presence of Apollo. The wrecks on the right are the remnants of the defeated enemy fleet, and the three figures are taking part in the procession to celebrate the victory. The relief is said to have been found in Avellino east of Naples and it presumably adorned the basis of a statue or an altar. The style indicates an origin from some years after the victory that marked the beginning of the Empire, but still under the reign of Augustus.

9. *Bust of a man*

10. *Roman historical relief*

Old Masters

THE ITALIAN SCHOOL

1. MASO DI BANCO: *The Coronation of the Virgin*

1. The *Coronation of the Virgin,* a painting by Maso di Banco, a pupil of Giotto, is one of the most distinguished of the collection of fourteenth-century works. The *Coronation of the Virgin,* together with two other panels (now at Chantilly and Berlin-Dahlem), was once part of a reliquary or tabernacle. A host of angels stand on either side of the simple, wide throne and below the steps leading up to it, playing musical instruments to celebrate the event. The clearly defined structure, the sense of space, and the summary shaping of the figures, all serve to emphasize the moment of the crowning. The delicately shaded colours, permeated with light, add a lyrical atmosphere to the Heavenly ceremony.

2. SPINELLO ARETINO: *St Nemesius and St John the Baptist*

2. Spinello Aretino was active in several Tuscan cities. It was in Lucca in 1385 that he painted the altarpiece for the Santa Maria Nuova cloister in Rome. The two saints are represented against a gilded background on the left panel, now in the Museum; the Roman tribune *Nemesius* is portrayed as a medieval knight in ceremonial robes, while *St John the Baptist,* the herald and faithful follower of Christ, is seen raising his hand in a prophetic gesture. Their strictly hieratic presentation is characteristic of the religious paintings of the second half of the fourteenth century, when the dynamic development of Tuscan painting, initiated by Giotto, came to a sudden halt. It is only in the scenes of martyrdom represented on the predella that this rigid solemnity gives place to an epic, narrative tone reminiscent of miniatures.

3. The small figures seen kneeling in the lower corners of the painting *The Mystic Marriage of St Catherine* represent the donors of the altarpiece, the saddler Jacopo di Tommaso and his wife. The predella illustrates the main episodes from the life of the saint in a lively and colourful narrative style. The date on Giovanni dal Ponte's work is scarcely legible but would appear to be 1421, the period which saw the emergence of Renaissance art in Florence. The decorative linear handling, the pattern of the background and the gestures characterized by pathos are still within the late Gothic tradition, while the solemn monumentality of the principal figures indicates a new trend.

4. The altarpiece which Sassetta painted between 1423 and 1426 for the chapel of the Sienese guild of wool-weavers, the *Arte della Lana,* has been dispersed and parts of it now lie in seven different collections. The Budapest panel once part of the predella *St Thomas Aquinas before the Altar of the Virgin* shows the Dominican philosopher saint kneeling in prayer before the altar. Sassetta, active in Siena in the fifteenth century, was an exponent of the latest achievements of Florentine painting and was able to place the saint in a spatial composition constructed with exact foreshortening. The space of the church is divided by slim pillars and arches, an atmosphere of holy calm is achieved by the use of pale colours while in the distance the representation of a fountain and a library evoke the silent and cloistered life of the monastery.

3. GIOVANNI
DAL PONTE:
*The Mystic Marriage of
St Catherine. Episodes from
the Legend of St Catherine*

4. SASSETTA:
*St Thomas Aquinas before
the Altar of the Virgin*

5. MICHELE PANNONIO: *Thalia*

5. This panel, painted by Michele Pannonio between 1456 and 1459, combines a taste for the late Gothic with an awareness of the new style of the Renaissance. *The Muse Thalia* is the Muse of Agriculture represented as the goddess of abundance enthroned, posed in a close-fitting robe which falls in loose folds over her knees, a garland of wheat on her head and flowers and a tendril of vine in her hand. On the pediment of the solid throne there are putti, with bunches of grapes, and on either side there are tall lilies in vases inlaid with precious stones. This is the only signed work of an artist who came from Hungary (Pannonia). It was one of a series of panels representing muses, designed for the study in Belfiore Castle near Ferrara, which was begun under the reign of Prince Lionello, but was completed only under Borso d'Este.

6. ANDREA DEL VERROCCHIO: *Virgin and Child Enthroned with Five Saints and Two Angels*

6. The panel *Virgin and Child Enthroned with Five Saints and Two Angels,* was created for the high altar of the Church of San Domenico al Maglio in Florence. Vasari believed this to be an early work by the Florentine artist, Andrea del Verrocchio, and though this was questioned in past years, the attribution is again favoured by scholars. It is a work in which we can see most of the features of Florentine painting at the time—the religious awe of the saints, the sculptural strength of the drawing, the marked characterization, the convincing rendering of space, the antique motifs of the throne and the walls, the trees painted with naturalistic fidelity.

7. GIOVANNI BOCCATI: *Virgin and Child Enthroned with Four Saints and Angels*

7. Verrocchio's robust saints are embodiments of the humanist ideal of man, the heroes of faith. Here, in Giovanni Boccati's panel, *Virgin and Child Enthroned with Four Saints and Angels,* the saints are portrayed as sanctimonious old men, ascetics who spend their lives in fasting and prayer. Nor did the artist, who came from Camerino, attempt to apply the new geometrical knowledge of proportional representation in his depiction of space: he was content to follow empirical perspectives, while representing in the utmost detail the splendid pontificals and the inlaid marble floor. A few decades after the completion of the work in 1473, the face of the Madonna was repainted by one of Pinturicchio's followers. This late, significant work, was created by Boccati as an altarpiece for the Chapel of St Sabinus in Orvieto Cathedral.

8. FILIPPINO LIPPI: *St Anthony of Padua Commends a Friar to the Patronage of the Virgin*

8. During the second part of the Florentine Quattrocento, both Botticelli and Filippino Lippi increasingly turned away from the naturalistic endeavours of their predecessors and the principles of rational pictorial composition. In their religious paintings, the vigorously arched contours are full of tension and are intended to express the intensity of mystical experience. In *St Anthony of Padua Commends a Friar to the Patronage of the* *Virgin,* an early panel by Filippino Lippi, the figure of the Madonna with the Child standing on her knee is depicted as a vision experienced by the Saint and the friar who has commissioned the paintings. The Madonna appears as if suspended, enthroned on clouds, only the hem of her robes billowing out to touch the flowery field. Her expression is melancholic as she looks down on the two figures appealing for protection.

9. Domenico Ghirlandaio's last work, the polyptych for the church of Santa Maria Novella in Florence, was finished by his pupils after the master's death in 1494. The altarpiece remained in its original place until 1804, when the panels were acquired separately by collectors. The Budapest wing depicting *St Stephen the Martyr* is of outstanding quality, thus not merely the preparatory sketch but the final execution of the figure can safely be attributed to Ghirlandaio. The gentle-faced young saint is represented with sure plasticity, framed by a niche with shell-shaped ornamentation. The figure is bathed in light which reveals the chiselled details of the face and hands and the beautiful folds of the brilliantly coloured robe.

9. DOMENICO GHIRLANDAIO: *St Stephen the Martyr*

10. CARLO CRIVELLI: *Virgin and Child Enthroned*

11. Giovanni Santi of Urbino, Raphael's father, modelled his work on that of Piero della Francesca, Melozzo da Forli and the Netherlandish artist, Justus van Gent, but in spite of his ready sympathy for innovation he could not achieve the ideal of proportional representation. His paintings lack harmony and it was only in his careful representation of surface detail that he equalled the great Renaissance masters. It is therefore his craftsmanlike depiction of details that lends an individual flavour to his few surviving paintings. The painting of *The Man of Sorrows,* damaged along the edges, represents Christ seated on His sarcophagus, surrounded by angels, pointing to His wounds. The fly painted on Christ's breast with striking verisimilitude is a motif of Netherlandish origin, a magic talisman supposed to keep away real flies.

10. In Carlo Crivelli's panel, *Virgin and Child Enthroned,* the Madonna is depicted with head bent self-consciously towards the Child, her eyes gleaming beneath lowered lids as she picks the stem of the apple with a fastidious gesture. The Child on her knee reaches with interest for the fruit. The details are highly decorative: the gold background, the antique marble throne, the Madonna's cloak, kerchief and veil, the curls framing the Child's face and the elaborately arranged folds of the Madonna's robe. It is the work of an artist whose imagination tends to the bizarre and the archaic. The polyptych, of which this is the central panel, was created for the church of S. Domenico at Ascoli Piceno. The wings are now in the National Gallery, London.

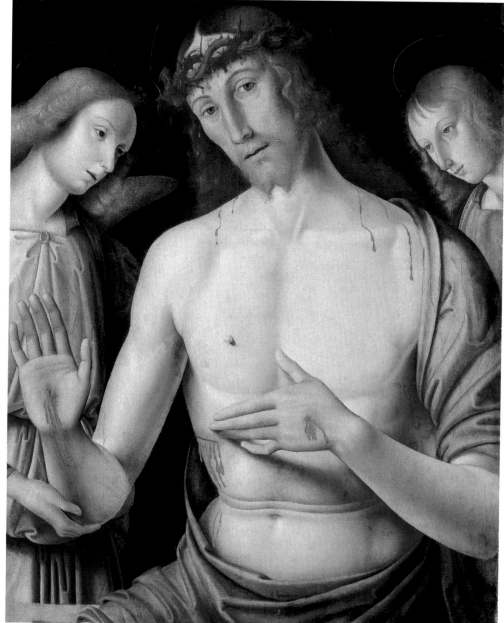

11. GIOVANNI SANTI:
The Man of Sorrows

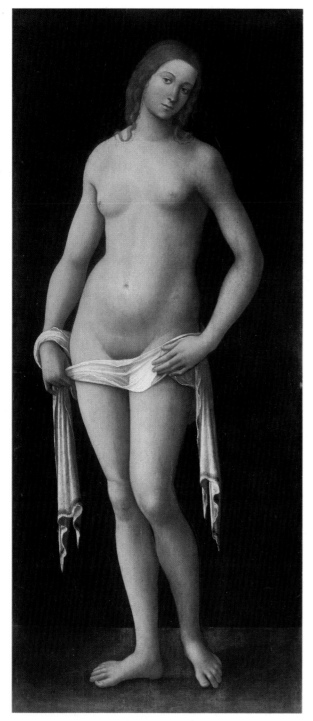

12. LORENZO COSTA: *Venus*

13. GIOVANNI ANTONIO BOLTRAFFIO: *The Virgin and Child*

12. The idealization of female beauty in the Italian art of the Renaissance was epitomized in the choice of Venus as a subject for painting. The goddess of beauty and love was also looked upon as the embodiment of truth and goodness and the personification of the Greek ideal of harmony. Botticelli's masterpieces, *Primavera* and *The Birth of Venus,* are the best known allegorical interpretations of the mythological goddess. Though there are no direct links between Botticelli and the Bolognese artist, Lorenzo Costa, this painting of *Venus* may owe something to the Florentine model. The figure is modelled in a firm, perhaps somewhat clumsy manner, but there is a hint of the great master's fluency in the light turn of the head which emphasizes the elegantly curving line of the body, outlined against a dark background.

13. Of the two paintings reserved in the Gallery of Old Masters by Giovanni Antonio Boltraffio, Leonardo's pupil in Milan, one was created as an altarpiece for the Cathedral at Lodi and is therefore known as the *Lodi Madonna.* The quality of this painting is inferior to that of his *Virgin and Child.* This striking difference in artistic quality lends support to the supposition of noted scholars that a considerable part of the execution of the latter panel can be attributed to Leonardo. The two figures leaning towards each other are placed in space in a masterly manner, and form a pyramidal composition. The rich folds of the silky sleeve, the delicately shaped face of the Child Jesus, His curly hair and the ornate earthenware vessel are all particularly fine details worthy of Leonardo's brush.

14. CORREGGIO: *The Virgin and Child with an Angel (Madonna del Latte)*

14. Correggio's *The Virgin and Child with an Angel (Madonna del Latte)* is related to Raphael's *Esterházy Madonna* only in its theme. The closed pyramidal composition gives place here to a more open, dynamic diagonal construction. The gestures, though resolved in both paintings, are here more lively and less formal, Raphael's restrained emotion becomes unrestrained sentimentally, and instead of the clear colours of Raphael's work we find tones richly shaded by the *sfumato* favoured by Leonardo. The softly modelled details are now submerged in shade and now bathed in light, evoking the illusion of movement and mystery. As we look at this masterpiece dating from the 1520s, it is easy to understand how Correggio, the master of the High Renaissance from Parma, could become one of the principal models for Baroque painters.

15. Like the portrait of the Prince of Urbino in the Uffizi the *Portrait of Pietro Bembo* is one of Raphael's earliest portraits. The pose, not quite frontal, the "tight" pictorial arrangement, the fresh colours and the perceptible uncertainty as to the inclusion of the hands all indicate that Raphael had not yet broken with the traditions of Perugino and the conventions of fifteenth-century portraiture. The subject of the portrait has only recently been identified with certainty as the poet and humanist Pietro Bembo, a distinguished man of letters and a leading figure of the Cinquecento.

16. RAPHAEL (RAFFAELLO SANTI):
The Esterházy Madonna

16. Raphael painted *The Esterházy Madonna* at the end of his Florentine period, and it is therefore a later interpretation of the theme than his *Madonna with Goldfinch* in the Uffizi and *La Belle Jardinière* in the Louvre. It is an unfinished work, the figures of Christ and St John being shaped by only the lightest preliminary brushwork. Though small in size, the painting reveals the skill of a master, for it is a work in which there is a perfect synthesis of realism and idealization, movement and repose, the complex and the simple. A sunlit landscape with antique ruins provides the background for the group of figures which form a polyphonic composition of great harmony based on parallels and contrasts.

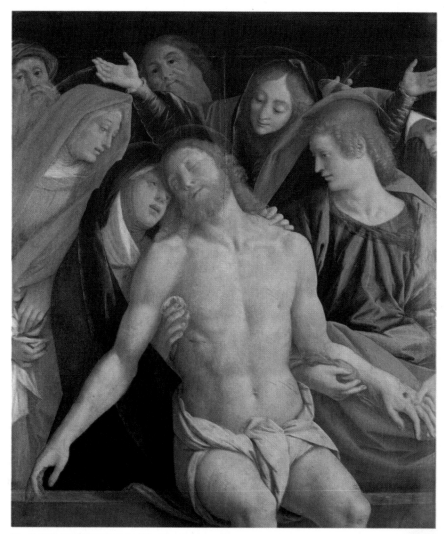

17. GAUDENZIO FERRARI: *The Lamentation*

19. The model in the *Portrait of a Man* attributed to Giorgione is shown touching his breast in a confessional gesture as he gazes broodingly into the distance. Only the face and hands are fully illuminated, the details being rendered in delicate tones. The identity of the painter is still uncertain, and there have been only tentative suggestions that the model was the poet Antonio Broccardo, who is mentioned in the inscription added later, but who was still a child around 1510 when the portrait was painted. There are also different interpretations for the emblems on the parapet. What is certain, however, is that this painting is a superb example of the new, lyrical style of portraiture introduced by Giorgione in Venice.

17. The art of Gaudenzio Ferrari has not yet received the recognition which is due to him, although he was undoubtedly a more individual and remarkable Renaissance painter than Leonardo's more widely known followers active in Lombardy. His panels are marked by a wealth of invention, fresh colours, vigorous composition, emotional spontaneity and a formulation of animated scenes, all contributing to a spectacular overall effect. All the virtues of his best paintings are present in *The Lamentation* from the late 1520s. The painting must have been highly praised, for records show that it was purchased in 1606 by Prince Vincenzo Gonzaga I.

18. The portraiture of the Venetian Quattrocento is represented by Gentile Bellini's *Caterina Cornaro, Queen of Cyprus,* possibly dating from 1500. The inscription on the tablet painted in the upper left hand corner of the picture records the names of the subject and the artist. The queen, who after the death of the King of Cyprus abdicated her throne in favour of the Republic of Venice (1489), was also represented by Giovanni Bellini's older brother in his panel entitled *The Miracle of the True Cross* (Accademia, Venice). In this portrait the features of the Venetian noblewoman are depicted in the linear, graphic manner typical of the master, who also shows the accuracy of a chronicler in his painting of the details of the costume studded with pearls and gems.

18. GENTILE BELLINI: *Portrait of Caterina Cornaro, Queen of Cyprus*

19. GIORGIONE: *Portrait of a Man*

20. SEBASTIANO DEL PIOMBO: *Portrait of a Man*

20. In the Museum there are three paintings by Sebastiano del Piombo, each representing one of his three creative periods. His *Portrait of a Man* must date from soon after he settled in Rome in 1511. Until the late nineteenth century the portrait was attributed to Raphael. The poetic mood of the landscape and the mysterious expression on the face of the anonymous young man still reflect the Venetian influence while the architecture dividing the pictorial space, the dignified pose and the uniform dark patch of the cloak with a fur collar indicate that the artist had quickly adapted to a new environment and was able to adapt his style to suit the taste of his new patrons, members of the Roman aristocracy.

21. TITIAN (TIZIANO VECELLIO): *Portrait of the Doge Marcantonio Trevisani*

21. Titian painted the *Portrait of the Doge Marcantonio Trevisani* in 1533 as one of a series of portraits for the Doge's Palace. The original canvas mentioned in documents was destroyed in a fire in the Great Council Chamber in 1577, but the surviving replica is in all probability the work of Titian. In all his portraits, including the Budapest likeness, the characterization is superb and the pictorial quality first rate. The weary, embittered expression is very moving and so realistic are the details that one can almost touch the heavy brocade coat shot with gold, the soft red velvet robes and the loosely folded kerchief in the Doge's hand.

22. *The Madonna with Child* by Girolamo Romanino of Brescia has an invisible third character: the Child Jesus turns to look at him, and Mary, suckling the Child also turns her beautiful, irregular face towards him as well. This genre motif enables the painter to break with convention and to create, even in a scene which had been portrayed on countless canvases before him, a new atmosphere of tension and mystery. In its broad sweeping style Romanino's impasto brushwork follows Venetian models.

The dark green curtain, the blue cloak with a leaf pattern, which captures the light and is richly folded in Baroque style over Mary's arm, as well as the russet dress all contribute to a colour scheme of soft, warm tones.

23. *The Sleeping Apollo and the Muses* by Lorenzo Lotto is a mythological idyll representing Apollo sleeping under the laurels on Parnassus as the Muses disperse in the glade, leaving behind their robes and the symbols of their art; so Fame also flies away. The story is not taken from the classics; it is probably a reference to the decline of the arts in the Middle Ages, before the rise of Humanism, but it could also be a mischievous criticism of a wealthy but ungenerous patron. The canvas dates from the 1540s, and the painter himself mentioned it in his account book on three occasions. In the seventeenth century the right-hand side of the canvas was damaged, and the picture lost from its original size.

22. GIROLAMO ROMANINO: *Madonna with Child*

23. LORENZO LOTTO: *The Sleeping Apollo and the Muses*

24. Although much of Giovanni Battista Moroni's work was commissioned by the Church, he was, first and foremost, a master of portraiture. This *Portrait of a Man* is a late work from 1575. The model is posed, as in most of Moroni's portraits, in a natural manner, with no show of ostentation or rhetoric. The man wears a red doublet in the Spanish fashion and is depicted leaning against a stone pillar, turning towards the spectator; behind him there is a green and brown wall. The inscription names the model as Jacopo Contarini, the Podestà of Padua, but this identification has not been authenticated. However, it is probable that the model was a member of the Venetian patrician family of the same name.

25. Ovid's story of *Hercules Expelling the Faun from Omphale's Bed* is vividly illustrated in this dramatic painting by Jacopo Tintoretto, the Venetian genius of the Late Renaissance. The central theme is represented in the middle distance, the supporting characters being placed diagonally in unstable postures, gesturing wildly.
The flickering light of the torches enhances the mystery of the action. According to the seventeenth-century biographer Carlo Ridolfi, the picture was one of four paintings each one of which represented a scene from the Hercules myth. It was commissioned by the Emperor Rudolph II who was an avid collector of mythological paintings with an element of the erotic.

24. GIOVANNI BATTISTA MORONI:
Portrait of Jacopo Contarini (?)

25. JACOPO TINTORETTO: *Hercules Expelling the Faun from Omphale's Bed*

26. Paolo Veronese, who liked to place his figures within scenes of pomp and ceremony or make them participants of spectacular plays, and who covered his huge canvases with easy brilliance and inexhaustible invention, applied the same ingenuity to his portraits. His *Portrait of a Man,* the youth wearing an ermined mantle, is seen in a posture of provocative self-assurance, standing before a wall overgrown with ivy, and a looped curtain, a feature later adopted in many Baroque portraits. The theatrical effect is further enhanced by the background in which ruins are outlined against an overcast sky. The painting has a fresh and picturesque quality, and the loose brushwork makes one feel as if Veronese had just lifted his *Portrait of a Man* from the easel.

27. Jacopo da Ponte embarked on his career in the small town of Bassano in Veneto, yet his sensitive reactions to the pictorial trends of his day saved him from provincialism. His work shows the influence of the great Venetian masters and the North Italian Mannerists. *Christ Collapses under the Cross* dates from around 1550 and is one of Bassano's principal works. The crowd of tortuous and moving figures, the contrast between the brutal soldiers and the grieving women, the noble and beautiful Veronica, the ominously flickering lights and a sense of the inevitability of Christ's death all serve to heighten the dramatic tension of the scene.

26. PAOLO VERONESE:
Portrait of a Man

27. JACOPO BASSANO:
Christ Collapses under the Cross

28. AGNOLO BRONZINO:
The Adoration of the Shepherds

28. Agnolo Bronzino, court painter to Prince Cosimo Medici, was obsessed by the pursuit of perfect form. In his *Adoration of the Shepherds* we find features of Mannerism such as the precision of outline, the ivory smoothness of forms, the enamelled colouring, the cold light of the moon, the elegance of the gestures and the classical, noble features of the characters. As it dates from before 1540, the panel is still free from the rigid academicism that characterized many of Bronzino's late compositions. The contemporary biographer Giorgio Vasari describes the panel as being of unique beauty, and its popularity is also borne out by the many surviving copies.

29. GIROLAMO MACCHIETTI: *Virgin and Child with St Anne*

29. In Girolamo Machiettis's *Virgin and Child with St Anne,* the figures give the impression of a giant sculptural group, of creatures gesturing with affection and wearing garments that are quite unrealistic in texture. A slender woman stands in the open doorway at the top of a staircase, Joseph turns back to her from a lower step, a youth is leaning on the balustrade looking outwards to a distant landscape with ruins, all contributing to create a dream-like scene in which Mary, the Child and St Anne are the principal characters. The artist has clearly been influenced by Pontormo, Parmigianino and Michelangelo. The work is a typical example of Late Mannerism which, during the period 1570–1590, became increasingly hermetic and permeated with nostalgia for the rich traditions of the Renaissance.

30. In *Venus Mourning Adonis,* Furini has made use of all the dramatic possibilities in the *chiaroscuro* associated with the name of Caravaggio. He was active in Florence, but his art was more individual than most of his contemporaries. This painting, executed for Giovanni Battista Baccelli, is one of Furini's earliest representative canvases, from about 1625–1630. The restlessness created by the use of exaggerated light and shade, the immoderate animation of the figures and the details taken from ancient sculpture (statues of Laocoon and Patroclos), the erotic element introduced by the partial nudity of the sophisticated female figures, all serve to express a singular ideal of beauty reflecting the taste of a decadent, cultivated yet introverted society.

30. FRANCESCO FURINI: *Venus Mourning Adonis*

31. Along with Caravaggio, Annibale Carracci is recognized as a supreme exponent of Italian Baroque. Born in Bologna, in 1595 he settled in Rome, where he produced works which summarized and further developed the traditions of the Italian Renaissance. He retained the perfect forms of the High Renaissance, applied colour like the great Venetian artist, used his knowledge of ancient sculpture and at the same time worked by directly observing nature, and so he was able to create a new, harmonious ideal of beauty, which for two hundred years continued to exercise a lasting influence on Italian paint-

ing and on European art in general. *Christ and the Woman of Samaria* dates from around 1595. The positioning of the heavy, monumental female figure evokes the Renaissance obsession with *contraposto* and provides a focal point for the composition; she is linked with the other figures by a series of expressive, rhetorical gestures in the Baroque style. The figures and the landscape elements unite to give a balanced composition. The rich Venetian colours have been deliberately chosen to express the artist's vision of idealized natural forms.

32. GUERCINO: *The Scourging of Christ*

32. Guercino, born in Cento, received his training in the academic tradition of Bologna. Nevertheless in his early works he achieved a dramatic effect by the use of light and shade and his figures were characterized by pathos in the popular style features indicating his response to the endeavours favoured by followers of Caravaggio. The influence of this early, dynamic period of Guercino was to be felt in the eighteenth century in Giuseppe Maria Crespi's stylistic innovations. It was while staying in Bologna in 1644 that Guercino was commissioned by the Berengani family to paint *The Scourging of Christ* for a church in Vicenza. The restrained use of gestures and light indicates a modification of the passionate interpretations of his youth, and the vertical emphasis of the composition indicates a development from a dynamic to a more static style. In this canvas he draws our attention, with the gentle lyricism inspired by Guido Reni, to the mental suffering of the humiliated Redeemer rather than to the physical brutality of the soldiers.

33. Bernardo Strozzi of Genova, who spent the last fifteen years of his life working in Venice, is one of the greatest North Italian painters of the first half of the seventeenth century. The style of his early period was determined by Mannerist antecedents and *tenebroso* endeavours, but after seeing paintings by Rubens and the Venetian masters, he began to use brilliant colours heavily impasted by means of free brushwork. Together with Fetti and Liss he greatly contributed to a new appreciation of the Baroque traditions of northern Italy and to the development of seventeenth-century Venetian painting. The light, tawny colours indicate that *The Tribute Money* dates from his Venetian period of the 1630s. Christ and the figures surrounding Him are posed with the pathos of the "grande maniera". The artist has devised a series of vehement rhythmic movements to create this animated but well-balanced composition.

33. BERNARDO STROZZI:
The Tribute Money

34. DOMENICO FETTI (?): *Sleeping Girl*

34. Domenico Fetti of Mantua was greatly influenced by the work of all the artists he saw during his journeys between Rome and Venice. From the northern artists he no doubt acquired his flair for popular genre scenes. His *Sleeping Girl* employs a simple, yet pictorially rewarding motif taken from life. The colours are delicate, the composition animated and the painting exemplifies the manner in which a competent artist can use everyday objects to create an enchanting work of art. It has recently been suggested that this painting may be the work of the Florentine Sigismondo Coccapanni.

35. Johann Liss, born in Holstein, travelled in the Netherlands and France before settling in Italy. The works he produced during his brief career are characterized by a highly individual fusion of the art of the North and the South. By means of unrestrained handling and a sensitive use of light and shade to resolve outlines, he developed still further the endeavours of the masters of the Flemish and Venetian Renaissance. His paintings were a source of inspiration to his contemporaries, his direct successors and even to the eighteenth-century painters, from Piazzetta to Tiepolo and Fragonard. *Judith with the Head of Holofernes* dates from his Venetian period, in the 1620s. The sharp contrast of light and shade stems froms his early interest in Caravaggio; the direction of the illumination creates the circular motion of the composition with its emotional effect. It is an unusual and innovatory interpretation of the story; her bloody deed accomplished, Judith is shown glancing coquettishly towards the spectator, thus introducing the grotesque element so often favoured by Liss.

36. *Bathsheba Bathing* is one of the principal works from Sebastiano Ricci's mature period. Considering its pictorial style, it may well have been painted in the 1720s, with its companion piece *Moses Defending the Daughters of Jethro*. In Bathsheba the painter has already abandoned his stylistic phase which foreshadowed the Rococo, and was again modelling his work on the light, colourful, well-balanced compositions of the Venetian masters of the Late Renaissance. The figures are grouped as if for a frieze: rather loosely yet producing an effect that is forceful as well as decorative. The noble forms, sparkling silvery light and soft hues create a festive mood. The shape and size of the painting indicate that the two companion pieces were intended for the walls of a large room in a Venetian palace.

35. JOHANN LISS: *Judith with the Head of Holofernes*

36. SEBASTIANO RICCI: *Bathsheba Bathing*

37. As a representative of the School of Bologna, Giuseppe Maria Crespi continued the traditions of the Italian Baroque which, like those of the Venetian Rococo, were maintained without a break for so many years. He reached back to academic tradition, and drew his inspiration from the Carraccis, but above all from Guercino's use of light and shade. His *Peasant Family Resting* has echoes of Rembrandt in the sincere and loving representation of simple people, a humanism accentuated by the restrained use of colour virtually reduced to monochrome, and the infinite delicacy of the light effects.

37. GIUSEPPE MARIA CRESPI: *Peasant Family Resting*

38. BERNARDO CAVALLINO: *Meeting of Joachim and Anne at the Golden Gate*

38. Bernardo Cavallino, a lyrical master of the Neapolitan school, usually painted quite small figures, and his *Joachim and Anne at the Golden Gate* is for him an unusually large canvas. The story comes from the *Apocrypha*. Joachim is seen in the background leaving Jerusalem with his flock after the priests have refused his sacrifice made in the hope that his wife might bear a child. But as he was praying in solitude an angel appeared to announce the birth of a daughter, Mary. In the foreground, Joachim is seen returning, to be embraced by his wife Anne at the Golden Gate of Jerusalem. Cavallino studied in the workshop of Massimo Stanzione, whose influence can be felt in the robust figures of Joachim and Anne and the contrasting colours of their garments in this youthful painting (from around 1640). The maid servant and the shepherd boy are types frequently seen in Cavallino's work. The background may have been painted by another member of the workshop, possibly Scipione Compagno.

53

39. GIOVANNI BATTISTA TIEPOLO: *St James the Greater Conquers the Moors*

39. Legend has it that the Apostle St James the Greater, who was buried in Santiago de Compostela, appeared in 844 at the Battle of Clavijo to support the Spaniards in their struggle to resist the advancing Moors. The last of the great Venetian painters of the eighteenth century, Giovanni Battista Tiepolo, worked at the Spanish court in the last years of his life. According to recent research, however, he was commissioned to paint the canvas *St James the Greater Conquers the Moors* while still in Venice, presumably in 1759, the Spanish ambassador to London. The work exhibits the finest virtues of the master's illusionistic fresco-like style. There is a nobility, monumentality and dynamism in the composition, which together with the brilliant colours exercise a powerful effect on the spectator. However, the decorativity is not a hollow device, but is employed to enhance the religious and dramatic significance; this is also evident in the ecstatic expression of the saint.

40. BERNARDO BELLOTTO: *The Kaunitz Palace and Garden in Vienna*

40. Bernardo Bellotto was commissioned by the Empress Maria Theresa in 1759–1760 to paint a series of the palaces of Vienna, which may have included *The Kaunitz Palace and Garden in Vienna*. This harmonious composition, with its prospect of the sunlit garden and its warm colours, is a superb example of *veduta* painting, the genre originating in Venice. Bellotto, the nephew of Canaletto who is sometimes referred to by the same name, is a representative of the second generation of *veduta* painters. As required by the genre, his view of Vienna is topographically correct—with the Church of Mariahilf to the left and the Charles Church and the Belvedere in the distance. It was customary to place a group of portrait figures in the foreground: here they include Prince Kaunitz-Rietberg (1711–1794), once the owner of the palace. In the early nineteenth century the palace came into the possession of the Esterházy family and it was here that the Esterházy Gallery was first opened to the public in 1815. The building has since been pulled down and is now the site of the Esterházy Park.

41. SIMON VOUET: *Apollo and the Muses*

42. NICCOLÒ RENIERI (RÉGNIER): *Card-players*

41. Seventeenth-century French painting is closely linked with that of the Italian schools. Most French artists visited Italy and it was in Rome that Simon Vouet first came under the influence of Caravaggio's work. Later he became interested in the achievements of the Bolognese and the Venetian Schools and applied to his own work what he learned there. The panel *Apollo and the Muses* was painted after his return to Paris. The splendidly rounded figures are displayed emerging from draperies tumbling about them in deep folds. They are elegantly posed in a rhythmic group which together with the delicately ruffled movements of the draperies gives to the composition an atmosphere that is buoyant yet calm. The stylized details are introduced to enhance the suggestion of harmony and nobility.

42. In the seventeenth century, when artists began to travel widely through Europe, national styles were fused as never before. From the late sixteenth century onwards, painters were setting out in growing numbers for Rome, which consequently became a *venue* for encounters and the exchanges of the most varied trends. Caravaggio's revolutionary endeavours influenced the development of art internationally, being first adopted by the Northern masters who visited Rome and sometimes settled there. The contribution made by French artists was their psychological insight and emphasis on characterization. Niccolò Renieri (Regnier) painted his *Card-Players* before 1626. The effect of the flickering lights is to emphasize the porcelain-like smoothness of forms in the dark interior. The figures represent a group of contemporary Bohemians who, though seated in an inn for their own amusement and pleasure, seem to be burdened by serious thoughts and the knowledge that they are enjoying only a brief respite from the sorrows of life.

43. Hubert Robert was active in the second half of the eighteenth century and his chosen genre was the landscape, in which the magic of the Italian scenery was then finding new expression. Robert spent ten years in Italy, where he saw Panini's pictures of classical ruins, but he was even more influenced by the fresh pictorial approach of his travelling companion Fragonard and the Italian countryside with its ruins of a glorious era, long vanished. In the Budapest canvas *Antique Ruins* Robert applied this fresh approach with attractive results to a quite modest motif. The vibration of light and shade on the surface is painted with animated and flexible strokes of his brush, as if controlled only by a summer breeze. This picture has the informality of a sketch evoking the poetry and reassuring charm of the landscape.

44. JACQUES BLANCHARD: *St Jerome*

44. Jacques Blanchard is sometimes referred to as the "French Titian". His style is characterized by the influence of the French Early Baroque and a crude version of Venetian picturesqueness acquired from the work of Fetti also, and more especially, that of Liss, with whom the painter became acquainted in Venice in 1626. The monumental figure of his *St Jerome,* painted in 1632, recalls Guido Reni's saints but without the ascetic severity of the latter. The warm red drapery, soft, restless brushwork executed with sometimes leaves uncovered the upper part of the body, yet the vibrant shades of the flesh combine happily with the sweeping folds of the robes and the overall effect is of unity.

43. HUBERT ROBERT: *Antique Ruins*

45. CLAUDE LORRAIN: *Villa in the Roman Campagna*

45. Claude Gellée, a native of Lorraine, represents the classical tradition of French Baroque. Like Poussin, he settled in Rome, where he developed a "classical" version of landscape painting so that it was given the esteem previously reserved for figural forms. *Villa in the Roman Campagna* was painted for Prince Camillo Panfili, around 1646. The landscape is bathed in the gentle light of late afternoon, and the natural forms are arranged with reassuring lucidity, thus creating a sense of harmony and tranquility. The distant view of wooded hills is treated with a highly individual aerial perspective and an infinitely delicate intensification of the colours. These methods produced landscapes with a magical atmosphere, and a lyricism that may truly be described as Virgilian.

THE FLEMISH SCHOOL

46. *The Virgin with the Child Writing,* one of the masterpieces of Franco--Flemish art, has come down to us only through copies. The original composition was probably the work of André Beauneveu, the great master of International Gothic, for Jean de Berry. One of the most splendid copies of the original is *The Virgin and Child and Six Angels,* thought to have been painted by an unknown Westphalian master, originating from the region to which its greatest representative, Konrad van Soest, first introduced the French influence in the early 1400s. The Virgin is depicted here as the Queen of Heaven, surrounded by angels singing and playing musical instruments. She holds an ink pot with a pen in her right hand, and a small pen-holder is suspended from her wrist. The Child in a splendid silk brocade robe pulls violently His mother's mantle, attempting to reach the pen. In the Middle Ages the Virgin was also known as the patroness of clerks, poets and writers. The representation of the Infant with a pen is the prefiguration of Christ as a teacher. Unfortunately, the inscription on the banderole in His hand is no longer legible.

47. The pose of the Madonna standing and holding her Child derives from French cathedral sculpture and Franco-Flemish art and became much favoured in Cologne and in the Netherlands as the popular type of small picture used for private devotion. This panel by Petrus Christus dating from around 1450, *The Virgin and Child,* is modelled after a work by the painter's great predecessor Jan van Eyck executed for Jan de Vos. This panel lacks the richness of Van Eyck's painting, but in the (almost Italian) purity of the spatial effects and the nearly perfect representation of perspective it carries

47. PETRUS CHRISTUS: *The Virgin and Child*

further the achievements of Van Eyck. The meaning of the picture would have been clear to the contemporary spectator: the Virgin represents the "new Eve" who has redeemed mankind from the tormenting punishment of the Fall, while Jesus, with chrystal globe, the symbol of sovereignty in His hand, is the future ruler in the era that follows Redemption. The Child raises His hand in a blessing directed most probably towards a donor, for the Budapest panel is thought to have been part of a diptych.

46. WESTPHALIAN MASTER: *The Virgin and Child and Six Angels*

48. Early Netherlandish painting first flourished in the rich seaport of Bruges, where many artists found work, fame and wealth. Gerard David arrived in Bruges as a youth in the 1480s, having left the poorer northern provinces. After Memling's death he was for a long time the leading artist in Bruges. The Budapest *Nativity* is the only surviving panel of an altarpiece painted soon after his arrival in Bruges. His model, as for most Flemish Nativity scenes, was the *Bladelin Altar* of Rogier van der Weyden, in which the Virgin is seen worshipping the Infant. The shepherds lend an individual charm to the panel. The devout red-haired shepherd

49. HANS MEMLING: *Crucifixion*

boy, a mere child, recalls Hugo van der Goes' deeply moving figures. His peasant face is in sharp contrast to the "intellectual" countenance of the shepherd bending his knee in the foreground, usually taken to be a self-portrait. The main enchantment of the panel lies in the technical perfection so characteristic of early Netherlandish painting, and the strong colours infused with light. The background landscape beneath a cloudy sky marks the birth of Flemish landscape painting.

49. Born in Seligenstadt near Frankfurt-am-Main, Hans Memling was granted civic rights in Bruges in 1456. He had an exquisite command of colour, and transmitted the achievements of Van Eyck and Rogier van der Weyden in a more popular form. He enjoyed great popularity during his lifetime and maintained a large workshop for his many commissions. His last important masterpiece was the *Passion Altar* in Lübeck, completed in 1491, of which the painting now in Budapest is a smaller version, presumably made for private devotion. The central panel of the triptych was discovered in a Hungarian collection in the early nineteenth century, while the wings came to Budapest from the Imperial Treasury in Vienna in 1934. The composition of the *Crucifixion* is strictly geometrical, the figures being arranged symmetrically in a semi-circle around the Cross. The drama is narrated through the gestures of the hands, but on the whole the representation lacks true dramatic force. The figures exhibit cool elegance. Dramatic rendering was in fact alien to Memling, and in this he could not approach the quality of his master and ideal, Rogier van der Weyden.

50. BAREND VAN ORLEY:
The Emperor Charles V

50. Charles, the son of Philip the Handsome and Johanna the Mad of Castile, was born in 1500 in Gent. In 1519 he was elected Holy Roman Emperor as Charles V. He spent his youth in Flanders and must have been 15 or 16 years old when Barend van Orley painted this portrait of him. The likeness of one of the greatest historical personalities of the sixteenth century is an important historical document and also an outstanding example of Flemish Renaissance portraiture. The painter presents the energetic, resolute youth in a bold composition. The elaboration of the details does nothing to detract from the portrayal of his character—neither the splendid apparel, the chain of the Order of the Golden Fleece, nor the wide-brimmed hat adorned with jewels. The hat still shows the Burgundian device of Charles the Bold. Barend van Orley was the court painter in Brussels for the energetic Habsburg Regents of the Netherlands, Margaret of Austria and Queen Mary of Hungary. He had never been to Italy and yet was the first representative of Renaissance style in his own country. In this early masterpiece he achieved a felicitous blend of the traditional realism of Flemish portraiture and the *grandezza* of Italian painting.

51. JOOS VAN CLEVE:
The Virgin and Child

51. The Italian historian Guiccardini wrote in 1567 of Joos van Cleve of Antwerp that: "he was outstanding particularly in his colouring and his painting after nature". His over-refined *Virgin and Child* was intended to be an object of private devotion in the house of a well-to-do burgher. One recognizes the influence of Leonardo da Vinci in the Virgin's smile, the delicate *chiaroscuro* on the faces and on the body of the Child; even the play of the hands recalls Leonardesque forms. Leonardo's influence had reached the Netherlands at a very early date, but it is also possible that Joos van Cleve had been to Lombardy; this is certainly indicated by his style. The Budapest painting is Italianate in its composition and architectural details. However, the landscape background and the disguised symbolism are elements of the Flemish tradition. The red wine in the Venetian glass refers to the blood of Christ and His sacrifice.

52. PIETER BRUEGEL THE ELDER: *St John the Baptist Preaching*

52. Pieter Bruegel the Elder painted *St John the Baptist Preaching* in 1566, a year after his *Labour of the Months*. Dated and signed, the Budapest painting has survived in an excellent state of preservation. It is a monumental and dynamic composition resembling the pictures of the *Months* in Vienna, featuring a diagonal line from the tree trunk on the left to the group in the upper right corner. The main subject of the painting, however, is neither the landscape nor Christ and St John the Baptist, but the crowd. It is a traditional subject in Flemish painting, but in this work Bruegel has reversed the meaning: the protagonists of the

Biblical story are nearly lost in the motley and colourful crowd. However, even the faces of those standing in the foreground are turned away from the spectator. The painting originated in calamitous times and probably conveyed a hidden message disguised as a Biblical subject. (It is no accident that nearly twenty copies of the panel are known.) This was the period when itinerant preachers were promulgating not only the new Faith but also the idea of political freedom in Flanders. Secretly and illegally they preached in the forests: this scene of a Biblical story had an allegorical meaning and conveyed a message to his contemporaries.

53. CORNELIS ENGEBRECHTSZ:
Portrait of a Man and a Woman
(probably *St Cecilia and Her Betrothed, Valerius*)

53. Cornelis Engelbrechtsz, active in Leyden, was a master with an interesting and individual touch. The small painting dating from around 1520, *Portrait of a Man and a Woman* (probably *St Cecilia and Her Betrothed, Valerius*) gives an idea of the early golden age of Dutch painting. In the sixteenth century the fusion of religious and profane subjects in painting was frequent. This small *tondo* was intended for the bedstead of a middle-class home. It depicts a legendary couple, Valerius and his wife, daughter of a Roman patrician, Cecilia, the patron saint of music. Having adopted Christianity, she converted her pagan bridegroom on the day of their wedding, and so instead of a happy marriage they looked forward to a martyr's death. They became symbols of the ideal marriage. The saints are portrayed here in the likeness of the couple who commissioned the work. The melancholic expression on the man's face is particularly arresting, whereas the young woman's face is more conventional, her long hair floating in the wind, her apparel and pose suggesting elegance and refinement.

54. SIR ANTHONY VAN DYCK: *St John the Evangelist*

54. Like Rubens, Sir Anthony van Dyck was one of the greatest masters of Flemish Baroque. They were, however, very different both in character and as artists. Van Dyck was scarcely more than fifteen years old when he had already acquired a workshop of his own in Antwerp. His series of Apostles painted between 1615 and 1616 is one of his earliest works and *St John the Evangelist,* one of the finest of the series. The artist followed early Flemish tradition by representing the saint in a red mantle, who blesses the cup of poison with the ritual gesture of a priest. Like the other figures in this series, it is a character study painted from a model, that is "from life". The same model can be seen in other paintings by Van Dyck. The explosive influence of Caravaggio's art in Flanders is also borne out by this early work of Van Dyck: in his handling of light he essentially follows the Italian master's style according to the fashionable Flemish "receipt" – warm tones seen in the light of a candle. Van Dyck painted several series of half-length portraits of the Apostles, which however were not intended for churches. They were bought by collectors in Antwerp as paintings of "famous men" from the Bible.

55. PETER PAUL RUBENS and SIR ANTHONY VAN DYCK: *Mucius Scaevola before Porsenna*

55. The theme of this painting from the workshop of Peter Paul Rubens, leading master of the Flemish Baroque, is taken from Roman history. Patriotism, courage and self-sacrifice are the virtues celebrated here. The canvas exhibits the hand of Rubens' most gifted pupil, Van Dyck, who worked together with the master between 1617 and 1621 and whose *Christ Carrying the Cross,* made for the Church of St Paul in Antwerp, features the back view of the twisted figure of a man on the right of the composition. The warm red and the handling of the light, floating draperies also point to Van Dyck's style. A sketch of this composition by Rubens is now in the Kupferstichkabinett in Berlin. In the seventeenth and eighteenth centuries many oil sketches and copies of various sizes were made. Its popularity may also have been enhanced by the fact that from 1636 until at least 1700 it was in the royal collection in Madrid. In the second half of the eighteenth century it was acquired by Chancellor Kaunitz in Vienna, and in 1820 it passed to the Esterházy Collection.

56. The third most notable personality of the School of Antwerp was Jacob Jordaens, who painted large altarpieces, mythological and allegorical compositions and striking portraits. His forceful, realistic portrayal of characters, his full-blooded humour and decorative style are deeply rooted in Flemish tradition. Although his work did not remain untouched by Rubens' influence, he retained his individual style. *The Fall of Man* dates from his mature period around 1630. There is no suggestion of drama in the scene: Eve plucks the forbidden fruit with an expression conveying only mild curiosity, while Adam, if a little fearful, seems resigned to the inevitable. The realistic nakedness of the figures was hidden beneath over-painting in Biedermeier style some time during the nineteenth century, but the picture has now been restored to its original condition. The earthly paradise is indicated by decoratively entwined plants in the foreground and various animals. The landscape background is thought to be the work of Jan Wildens.

57. The genre of *cabinet d'amateur* (the depiction of studios or picture collections), which was so popular among the Antwerp painters, is here transformed by Frans Fancken into an allegorical composition. The female artist is working on a painting of the Nativity in a workshop. She personifies the Christian soul experiencing a vision of Christ, haloed and exhibiting His open heart. The solemn mood is further enhanced by the orchestra of angels supported by clouds; the assistants working with clay and mixing paints are also angels. In the background there are the five wise virgins, and in a far recess St Anne and the Virgin. The paintings propped around the workshop are all examples of *The Imitation of Christ,* that is, religious painting. Some of them refer to Christ's humility and His suffering, for instance a statuette of the *Crucifixion,* an *Ecce Homo,* the *Mater Dolorosa* on the table, the picture *Christ Washing His Disciples' Feet, Christ Scorned* and the *Agony in the Garden.* Other paintings refer to the protective role of the Church *(The Good Shepherd)* and there are sculptures arranged on a shelf representing the Christian virtues of Faith, Hope and Love. Most prominent of all is the painting of the Last Judgement placed like an altar behind the cross.

56. JACOB JORDAENS: *The Fall of Man*

57. FRANS FRANCKEN THE YOUNGER:
The Imitation of Christ

58. Of the Flemish landscape painters it was Jan Wildens who most successfully applied to his own work the lessons learned from Rubens. This was the result of close cooperation with the master in his work, and also the ties of friendship which were later strengthened by family ties. His *Landscape with Farm* is thought to date from 1629 and is one of his finest works. It is a large composition, decorative yet realistic, a rendering in lively colours of a landscape in which we sense the calmness after a storm.

58. JAN WILDENS: *Landscape with Farm*

59. FRANS HALS: *Portrait of a Man*

59. Frans Hals joined the Haarlem Painters' Guild in 1610, and it was not long before he was painting portraits of members of an expanding middle-class. His fresh likenesses, often combined with genre elements, represent a singular field of Baroque portraiture. His large conversation pieces are outstanding examples of this specific Dutch genre. The secret of his forceful characterization lies in a spontaneous simplicity and, despite the compulsory externals, an informality in his depiction of the sitter. The *Portrait of a Man,* dating from 1634, represents a somewhat sensual young man, half-smiling and wearing a formal black and white costume. The artist has used broad, quick strokes of the brush to outline the forms, represent the texture of the materials and create a sense of space.

60. One of the first generation of Dutch genre painters, Buytewech, was active in Haarlem and Rotterdam, and his life's work forms a link between Late Mannerism and the seventeenth-century trend towards the imitation of nature. His drawings, varied in subject, greatly influenced his younger contemporaries, while his few surviving paintings initiated a type of allegorical and moralizing composition with lifelike figures in realistic settings. In *A Merry Company* we can see symbols of the five senses—the pipe for the sense of smell, the burning candle for sight, the jug and glass for taste, the musical instruments for hearing and the brazier for the sense of touch. The three elegant youths are the guests of Lady World, who personifies worldly pleasures —indicated by the map on the wall. The monkey too is a traditional symbol of sinful sensuality. The affected posture of the figures dressed in the fashion of the 1620s, along with their rigid gestures, show that the painter used dummies as models.

61. The scene in *St Peter's Denial of Christ* is transmuted in Jan Miense Molenaer's composition and we are shown the interior of a tavern. The real meaning of the painting is revealed only by the cock seen through the open door to the right through which Peter, depicted as a frightened old man, is trying to escape. A pupil of Frans Hals, Molenaer, is an interesting representative of the Harleem School. His genre scenes, abounding in realistic detail, always conceal some moral which, in the course of the development of genre painting led to a semblance of realism. Molenaer's early works, including this painting dating from 1636, combine traditional iconography with a novel representation of reality.

60. WILLEM PIÉTERSZ. BUYTEWECH: *A Merry Company*

61. JAN MIENSE MOLENAER: *St Peter's Denial of Christ*

62. AERT DE GELDER: *Esther and Mordecai*

62. Aert de Gelder of Dordrecht was Rembrandt's most faithful pupil, who fully appreciated and followed his late style. Aert de Gelder portrayed characters from the Old Testament, almost life-size and usually half-length. He had a special gift for the representation of costly draperies, jewels and oriental objects. He painted several pictures of episodes from the Book of Esther, one of the most harmonious being *Esther and Mordecai,* dating from 1685. The essence of the story is caught in this representation of the tense moment of decision when the heroine, yielding to her foster father's persuasion, undertakes to intercede with the king to save her people. The drama of the moment is emphasized by the use of fiery colours, strong contrasts of light and shade and broadly impasted brushwork.

63. Rembrandt's sketch for *The Dream of St Joseph,* painted in the 1650s in his Amsterdam workshop, which is now in the Kupferstichkabinett in Berlin, served as the basis for the work by the master. It seems very probable that in this painting the master was assisted by his talented pupil, Barent Fabritius. The warm, brown colours of the night scene are enlivened by the visionary figure of the angel, the source of light illuminating the figures. The essence of Rembrandt's interpretation of Biblical scenes was his emphasis on the humanity of the protagonists. Instead of pointing to the moral of the story he creates the impression that these events can happen to anyone at any time. It is for this reason that his paintings, expressing his own sympathy and insight, are valued by each succeeding generation.

63. REMBRANDT HARMENSZ. VAN RIJN: *The Dream of St Joseph*

64. Adriaen van Ostade, whose genre scenes with peasants were the most popular of their kind, was at first influenced by Frans Hals. In his paintings of everyday scenes he created an iconography and artistic idiom of his own. In his early work he represented animated scenes of peasants carousing, reminiscent of Brouwer; later, influenced by Rembrandt, he painted first interiors in tawny shades, then more colourful genre scenes characterized by a rich narrative vein. *The Fishwife,* now in Budapest, represents his late period and presumably dates from after 1672, when he had already painted a version of the same subject, which is now in the Rijksmuseum in Amsterdam.

65. Jan Steen's genre scenes of prosperous families indulging in uproarious gaiety perhaps reveal more clearly than any other the Dutch national character. But for the seventeenth-century spectator his Biblical, mythological and genre scenes provided not only a feast to the eye and reflections of the pleasant occasions of their daily life, they also conveyed moral lessons.

A Merry Company is also known by the title *The Cat Family,* and within this scene of family carousal are symbols of the five senses, the source of earthly pleasures. The stroking of the cats stands for touch, the carousal for taste, the dog for the sense of smell, the music-makers for hearing and the head of the family depicted reading aloud, a self-portrait, symbolizes sight. But the skull in the background is a reminder of the evanescence of pleasure, while the owl on the left side of the painting refers to human blindness and stupidity.

66. Within the genre of still-life painting that developed in the Netherlands, the "monochrome" banquets of the Haarlem and Amsterdam Schools were particularly influential. They were responsible for the emergence of a singular type featuring depictions of smoking appliances, iconographically linked to Vanitas paintings and Lenten pieces exhorting self-moderation. Jan Jansz van de Velde's sensitively treated *Still-life,* with its delicate colours and light effects, is a fine example of the type. The crested earthen jug, a constant accessory in these pieces, probably refers to the fact that harmful passion of smoking which was rapidly gaining ground by the mid-seventeenth century, was recorded as "dry drunkenness" by the Dutch.

67. A basic feature of Dutch architectural painting of the mid-seventeenth century is its topographical accuracy. This is true of all such paintings whether townscapes or church interiors. Pieter Saenredam's accurate drawings enabled him to paint—sometimes after an interval of fifteen or twenty years—realistic pictures of buildings which in the intervening years may even have been destroyed as in the case of the picture of the old town-hall in Amsterdam. *Interior of the Nieuwe Kerk in Haarlem* was completed on August 16, 1653. This exact dating is also indicative of the artist's concern for accurate documentation, for this year he saw the completion of the construction work on the new church designed by Jacob van Campen, the most significant architect of the time. Saenredam's painting is noteworthy not only for the precision of the detail but also for a stemming from his rendering of the quality of the light, which is intensified by the purity of the Protestant Church.

66. JAN JANSZ.
VAN DE VELDE: *Still-life*

67. PIETER SAENREDAM:
*The Interior of the
Nieuwe Kerk in Haarlem*

68. In the 1630s, an essentially national feature of Dutch painting became evident in the trend towards simple themes in monochrome. Jan van Goyen, a pioneer of realistic depictions in Dutch landscape painting, settled in The Hague where his paintings of villages and scenes by the seashore stimulated others to paint these subjects. He also liked to paint rivers and canals, and later produced seascapes too. This small masterpiece, *Seascape with Fishermen,* creates the atmospheric effect of silvery grey clouds massed above a calm sheet of water stretching towards a low horizon.

69. The herd of cows in the foreground of this panel by Albert Cuyp, entitled *Cows in the Water,* are seen in the golden light of late afternoon. The level rays of the sun are reflected in the still waters of a river or estuary. To create this peaceful atmosphere of a summer afternoon the painter uses the device of backlighting so that the animals in the foreground are seen outlined against the pale sky above the low horizon. This treatment typifies his mature compositions from the 1650s onwards and it can be traced to the influence of the Utrecht exponents of Italianate landscape, for instance Jan Both. At the same time he follows in the wake of Jan van Goyen and Salomon van Ruysdael in his masterly rendering of the swirling clouds, the surface of the water and the misty air, misty atmosphere of the Dutch landscape. These idyllic landscapes by the Dordrecht master were particularly popular in England. He was also widely known as a painter of portraits and conversation pieces.

69. AELBERT CUYP:
Cows in the Water

70. JACOB VAN RUISDAEL: *The View of Binnenamstel in Amsterdam*

70. Jacob van Ruisdael was the most important of the Dutch landscape painters and treated the widest range of subjects – mysterious forests, fierce waterfalls, ruined palaces and graveyards, calm lakes, sunlit wheat fields, gloomy winter landscapes, seaports, windmills, watermills, and church towers. His pictures constitute an interpretation of the age in which he lived. The picture in the Museum, *View of the Binnenamstel in Amsterdam,* is more than a townscape seen in the light and shade of a fine afternoon, the buildings catching the light as the clouds disperse. There is tension and symbolism in the solitary figure approaching along the boldly conceived, deeply rutted cart track leading to a wooden fence which bars his way.

71. ALBRECHT ALTDORFER:
The Crucifixion

71. The bizarre archaic quality of Albrecht Altdorfer's *Crucifixion* creates the impression of a modern panel. Against a gold background, which in mediaeval paintings signified the pure light of Heaven, the artist has represented the cruel realities of an earthly tragedy. Altdorfer has introduced here a greater number of more powerfully armed soldiers than may be traditionally found in late mediaeval calvaries. The superior force and authority of the executioners is demonstrated by the abundance of arms, but they have no individuality and are a mere faceless crowd. In the foreground stand a group of large *repoussoir* figures, whose attitudes and proportions are different from those of the homogeneous crowd. The Virgin is supported by the Holy Women as she falls. St John the Evangelist stands on the right with his back to the spectator. Both groups derive from Mantegna's engravings, which frequently served as models for German painters. Altdorfer was a great and solitary figure in German Renaissance painting. This panel illustrates his skill in composing mass scenes. The panel was in St Florian Monastery, together with the master's important altarpieces, it was probably made for the domestic chapel of Peter Maurer some time between 1512, 1518 or 1520.

72. ALBRECHT DÜRER:
Portrait of a Man

72. Apart from his religious works, Albrecht Dürer painted chiefly portraits. He wrote on the mission of painting: "The art of painting is employed in the service of the Church... It preserves also the likeness of men after their death..." In this *Portrait of a Man* he introduces no objects to distract us, though clearly the man wearing a black mantle, his hair confined within a net, was one of the well-to-do burghers. The features are clearly defined and the artist conveys the impression of a friendly and open nature. The motif of the window reflected in the eyes and the use of the finest possible brush for painting the hair and the eyebrows are elements frequently employed in Dürer's portraiture. The faint smile linger-

ing on the compressed lips is also seen in Leonardo's works. (Leonardo's influence in Dürer's painting can already be seen in his works made before 1505.) The attribution of this painting is not unanimously accepted. Some scholars have recently ascribed it to Hans von Kulmbach or Hans Baldung Grien; these attributions, however, lead to further problems from the point of view of the latter painter's œuvre.

The identity of the sitter is also uncertain. It was believed to be Endres Dürer, the painter's younger brother, but more recently it has been put forward that the painting may be a youthful portrait of Hans Burgkmair.

73–74. It was Dürer who introduced the nude into German painting. Between 1503 and 1507 Hans Baldung Grien worked in Dürer's workshop, and must therefore have been familiar with his life-size pictures, *Adam* and *Eve,* completed in 1507. Dürer's classical, idealized nudes represent not only the protagonists of the Biblical story but the ideal of human body and perfect proportions. Baldung's *Adam* and *Eve* is the Mannerist antithesis of Dürer's style, well over life-size with their emphatic nudity combined with an affectation for modesty. Adam turns with an almost lecherous challenge towards the serpent with a woman's face, and his head and facial expression resemble an ancient statue of a satyr rather than a Biblical character.

Eve watches the dialogue between the two of them with a smile of complicity. The eroticism of this interpretation of the Fall is typical of the moralizing aspect of Mannerism. Baldung's painting was of course not intended for a church but for a patrician's home in Strasbourg, together with the figures of Venus and Judith, handled in a similar way. This coupling of Biblical and mythological figures was by no means unique in sixteenth-century German art; it signified the victory of sensuality over common sense. This masterpiece of Baldung's mature period dates from around 1524–1525.

75. LUCAS CRANACH THE ELDER:
The Mystic Marriage of St Catherine

75. Lucas Cranach the Elder, a contemporary of Dürer, court painter to the Elector of Saxony and a man of some wealth, was active in the spirit first of Catholicism and later of Reformation. *The Mystic Marriage of St Catherine,* dating from around 1516–1518, was probably intended for private devotion. Cranach painted several versions of this subject. The cult of St Catherine and St Barbara was also popular at the court, as relics of the two saints were preserved in Wittenberg. Together with St Dorothy and St Margaret, the saints are shown around the Virgin, who is wearing a simple robe and holding the Child on her knee. The formal focus of the composition, St Catherine's "mystic" marriage is here rendered as nothing more than a children's game. The scene resembles Italian *Sacra Conversazione* compositions, although the setting with the romantic Alpine mountains reminds us of Cranach's travels in Austria in his youth. The fashionable garments of the saintly virgins, and their pronounced worldly elegance and beauty recall the bold maids of honour at the Saxon court. Here again there is an uninterrupted fusion of the religious and the profane.

76. A celebrated member of the international society of artists and scholars in Naples and Rome, Angelica Kauffmann's paintings, especially her portraits, were much appreciated by her contemporaries, including Goethe.

She applied effectively and consistently the approach of the new trend of neo-Classicism, which, however, she blended harmoniously with Rococo traditions. The canvas, *Portrait of a Woman,* dating probably from 1795, is not a self-portrait as was formerly believed, but probably a likeness of Princess Esterházy posed by her dressing table as Venus. The subject, as well as the motif of the hand holding drapery, are of ancient origin, but a link with the Rococo may be seen in the ease of the execution on the folds of the robe, the colouring and the exploitation of pictorial effects.

77. The Austrian Franz Anton Maulbertsch was the most significant fresco painter of Central Europe in the eighteenth century. The largest number, and indeed the most significant of his works have survived in Hungary. The selection of his works in the Budapest Museum is representative of each stage of his career. *The Holy Trinity,* a colour sketch for an altarpiece, is a late work from the 1780s. Maulbertsch prepared many preliminary drawings and oil sketches for his frescoes and altarpieces. The freedom and spontaneity of these small sketches make them more attractive to present taste than the finished frescoes, which are more difficult to survey, having lost much of their original buoyancy.

This sketch is enchanting in its fresh, loose handling, the visionary representation of the subject suffused in light, the bright colours with a silvery sparkle, and the impressionistic approach.

77. FRANZ ANTON MAULBERTSCH: *The Holy Trinity*

76. ANGELICA KAUFFMANN: *Portrait of a Woman*

THE SPANISH SCHOOL

78. El Greco was the first important European master of "Siglo del Oro" painting. Born in Candia, Crete, in 1541, El Greco first studied in Venice between 1567 and 1570 and was later active in Rome. Like many of his Italian contemporaries, he then travelled to Spain, attracted by the possibilities in the ambitious architectural schemes initiated by King Philip II. There he settled in 1577 in Toledo. All his works now in Budapest were painted in Spain, one of the earliest being the *Magdalene,* presumably dating from around 1578–80. The range of colours—blue, green and golden yellows—still reveals the influence of the Venetian masters. But the picture is also characterized by the typical features of El Greco's mature art—the huge, visionary eyes, the elongated forms of the hand resting on a skull, the contrast between the lavender blue veil and the red hair, also the illumination of the figure and the mountainous background by a luminous glow emerging from a break.

The representation of the *Magdalene* is suffused with a lofty atmosphere of religious devotion, which from the 1580s onwards was enriched in El Greco's works by even greater expressive power. The painting was donated to the Museum in 1921 by the famous collector Marcell Nemes, one of those who initiated a new attitude to El Greco's art.

78. EL GRECO (DOMENIKOS THEOTOCOPOULOS): *Mary Magdalene*

79. EL GRECO (DOMENIKOS THEOTOCOPOULOS): *Study of a Man*

79. This singular *Study of a Man* by El Greco has been interpreted in many different ways by scholars. It has been taken both for a representation of St James the Greater, a study for a series of Apostles, even a self-portrait. The pose and character of the head, the garment and the details of the cloak relate it to the familiar representation of St James the Greater. El Greco painted his series of Apostles in the last quarter of his life, in the spirit of the Counter-Reformation, representing each saint as an individual with his own personality and temperament, as if painting portraits. The painting now in Budapest combines the manner of painting from a model with a profound insight into character. More like a sketch than a finished portrait, it is built up from tiny touches, in scintillating colours, against a background indicating the sky. It is presumably a study for the *Series of Apostles* in Almadrones in Guadalajara.

80. EL GRECO (DOMENIKOS THEOTOCOPOULOS): *The Agony in the Garden*

81. DIEGO RODRÍGUEZ DE SILVA Y VELÁZQUEZ: *Peasants Having a Meal*

80. In *The Agony in the Garden,* El Greco (the name by which Domenikos Theotokopoulos was known while still a student in Italy) has created a singularly concentrated representation of the Biblical story recorded in the Gospels. The composition falls into two spheres. In the upper field Christ experiences his vision of the angel, emerging from a heavenly glow which illuminates the figure of Christ and provides a nimbus around His head. The tree split asunder refers to the approach of death, while the olive-branch sprouting out of it is a symbol of hope and eternal life. In the lower half of the composition, the Apostles are shown sleeping, the strange harmony of the colours and light effects emphasizing the transcendent character of the scene. The composition includes a distant view of a group of soldiers accompanying Judas on their mission to seize Jesus; the townscape in the background is a reference to Toledo. This late masterpiece by El Greco, dating from around 1610–1614, is imbued with an expressive power motivated by the religious mysticism of the period.

81. The lively trading town of Seville was a cultural and economic centre in seventeenth-century Spain. The most famous masters of the Baroque tradition, Velázquez, Cano, Zurbarán and Murillo, were active for varying periods either in the city or elsewhere in Andalusia. Velázquez, the celebrated court painter of King Philip IV, spent his youth in Seville. His first experience with a *bodegón,* a kitchen scene with still-life elements, was probably in the workshop of Herrera the Elder. Between 1617 and 1623, Velázquez painted a number of such scenes in warm shades against a rusty background but when he moved to Madrid these gave place to his silvery court paintings. Relatively few works survive from his early period, one of them being the *Peasants Having a Meal,* probably dating from around 1618. The title is traditional, although the figures represent not peasants but poor nobles shown eating a frugal meal as in a story by Cervantes. The well-balanced composition, the lively relationship of the characters, also their gestures, all stress the conversational mood, and the free, mature handling indicates that the young master was employing a type with which he had already been familiar.

82. JUSEPE DE RIBERA: *The Martyrdom of St Andrew*

82. Spanish-born Jusepe de Ribera spent some years of study in northern Italy before settling in Naples in 1616. Soon he developed into one of the most noted masters, and from the 1620s onwards many young painters studied in his workshop. In his representations of martyrs, for instance, *The Martyrdom of St Andrew,* he eschewed the portrayal of horrors and concentrated on the moments before the martyr's death. In this canvas the Roman high priest is seen showing a statue of Jupiter to the saint, thus conveying that by agreeing to worship an alien god he would escape martyrdom. Ribera concentrates attention on the figure of the saint, whose body is illuminated by light, while the features of the executioners, the priest, the soldiers and the mourning woman in the background are partially glimpsed in the surrounding darkness. Occasional reds and ochres stand out from the dark brown and black ground colour typical of Ribera's early works, while the olive and ash-blue of the background testify to the enrichment of Ribera's palette. The inscription in a concise biography of the artist: "Ribera, the Spanish master from Valencia, Játiva, member of the Accademia in Rome, painted this picture in Naples in 1628."

83. In 1629 and in 1632–1633, Francisco Pacheco, Antonio del Castillo and Alonso Cano painted altarpieces for the Carmelite monastery of San Adalbert in Seville. At the same time, between 1630 and 1633, Francisco de Zurbarán painted his *St Andrew*—the patron saint of the Carmelites—for the monastery. Executed in sharply contrasting tones of blue, red and ochre, and delicately modelled to give a sculptural effect, this work is one of the most striking examples of Spanish tenebrism, that is, painting in a very low key. This painting, together with a great many other Spanish works of art, were sent to France by Marshall Soult, one of Napoleon's officers at the time of the French invasion.

84. FRANCISCO DE ZURBARÁN: *The Immaculate Conception*

83. FRANCISCO DE ZURBARÁN: *St Andrew*

84. Towards the end of his life, in 1658, Zurbarán moved to Madrid and it was there, in 1661, that he painted *The Immaculate Conception,* a popular theme in Spanish Baroque painting, and one which Zurbarán had already depicted several times. It was, in fact, the subject of his earliest painting, from 1616, the attribution of which is firmly established. The painting now in Budapest can be paralleled by a canvas with the same title now in the Musée des Beaux-Arts in Bordeaux. The Virgin is portrayed as the Queen of Heaven, hovering against a golden sky peopled with cherubs, and resting her foot lightly on the crystal globe of the universe surrounded by the heads of cherubs. Her floating blue mantle conveys a sense of movement. The motifs of the landscape, which emerges like a vision from the ash-blue and rose coloured clouds (mirror, tower, well, palm cypress), are the Virgin's symbols in the litany of Loreto. The painting was donated to the Hungarian state by Prince Miklós Esterházy in 1871.

85. Bartolomé Estéban Murillo, the most popular of the Spanish religious artists of the seventeenth century, painted *The Infant Jesus Distributing Bread to Pilgrims* for the Hospital de los Venerables (Home for Aged Priests) in Seville. The aged master was commissioned to paint this theme, highly suitable for the refectory, by Canon Justino de Neve. It has been assumed, though it is by no means certain, that the canon was the model for the pilgrim reaching for the bread. Certainly Don Justino de Neve was an admirer of Murillo's painting, and as one of the painter's friends, he was named Murillo's executor in his will. As one of the leading church dignitaries of Seville, the canon gave several commissions to Murillo. The unassuming dignity of the figure of the Madonna seen against a golden yellow background and the careful representation of the still-life details are typical of Murillo's late period. The altarpiece was taken to France by Marshall Soult, and it was purchased for the Esterházy Collection in 1822.

85. BARTOLOMÉ ESTÉBAN MURILLO:
The Infant Jesus Distributing Bread to Pilgrims

86. ALONSO CANO:
Portrait of the Infante Don Baltasar Carlos

86. According to Palomino, a biographer of Spanish painting, Alonso Cano was the drawing master of the Infante Don Baltasar Carlos, the son of King Philip IV and Elisabeth of Bourbon, who was born in 1629 in Madrid, and who died in 1646 in Zaragoza. Judging from the age of the child, the portrait must date from around 1634–1635. The painter Jusepe Martinez records that Cano, then still active in Andalusia, visited him in his Madrid home in 1634. It is possible that the *Portrait of the Infante Don Baltasar Carlos* was painted in that year. The posture of the child and the choice of landscape details reflect the influence of Velázquez, who had been a fellow apprentice in Seville. Cano was a distinguished sculptor and architect as well as a painter, and few of his portraits have survived. One of the earliest is this likeness now in Budapest. It was cleaned in 1981 so that we can now appreciate the silvery colours and the brilliant handling of the softly modelled figure, the plants and the tree. It is now possible to see even the *pentimenti,* the painter's own alterations to the position of the right arm and details of the hair and the costume.

87. Portraiture occupies an important place in Francisco de Goya's lifework. At the court of Charles IV, he painted members of the royal family and leading politicians of the day. He also painted likenesses of his friends, writers, poets, actors and popular *toreros*. Goya counted among his friends J. A. Ceán Bermúdez, a noted writer on art of the period. The portrait of *Señora Bermúdez* presumably dates from between 1780 and 1785. (The portrait of Ceán Bermúdez, taken to be a companion piece, is in a private collection in Madrid.) Goya found pleasure in painting the elaborate green costume and the dressed hair. The lady is represented as witty, though not very beautiful, she is seen to be free from any kind of self-conceit and one feels that there was an intellectual link between the artist and the sitter.

87. FRANCISCO DE GOYA: *Portrait of Señora Bermúdez*

88. FRANCISCO DE GOYA:
The Water Seller

88. Goya demonstrated from early youth onwards a flair for depicting popular characters. *The Water Seller* (Prado, Madrid) dating from 1791–1792 is in its theme a precursor of *The Water Seller (La aguadora)* now in Budapest. The figure of *The Knife-grinder* appears only once in Goya's art, but his *Blacksmiths* (New York, Frick Collection) is akin to it in content, style and the date of origin. The Budapest paintings are thought to date from around 1810. Some of Goya's paintings, owned by his widow, Josefa Bayeu, were subsequently bequeathed to his son Javier. An inventory of these, dated 1812, describes one of the paintings as "a water seller and its companion piece", most probably a reference to the paintings in Budapest. The fact that they were intended as companion pieces is borne out by their identical size, the representation of the figure from a slight bottom view, the similar colouring and treatment, and also by Goya's use of canvases previously selected for companion pieces. X-ray examination has revealed in both cases that the present surface covers still-lifes of flowers in broad-bellied, slim-necked vases. *The Knife-grinder* and *The Water Seller* were acquired for the Esterházy Collection in 1820 and 1822, after the auction of the Kaunitz Collection.

THE ENGLISH SCHOOL

89. By the eighteenth century, the growing prosperity of the middle classes enlarged the market for portraits. A new type of middle-class portrait was created by Hogarth, and as it developed in the hands of the English masters, it acquired a specifically national character. Sir Joshua Reynolds, although famous for his portraits of members of the aristocracy, continued this Hogarthian trend. *The Portrait of Admiral Sir Edward Hughes* summarizes his best virtues. It is painted in glowing colours as a picturesque representation of a successful member of the professional classes, the ruddy face indicating a partiality for good food and drink.

90. In the course of the eighteenth century, landscape painting assumed growing significance in England, though it was not until the end of the century that it assumed a uniquely national character. John Constable was perhaps the greatest exponent of English landscape painting. The small masterpiece entitled *Waterloo Celebrations at East Bergholt* is in the style of his brilliant sketches. It captures the glittering light of the uncertain weather and changing mood of a day in the English countryside, expressing the artist's own love for his native land and foreshadowing the style of the Impressionists.

89. SIR JOSHUA REYNOLDS: *Portrait of Admiral Sir Edward Hughes*

90. JOHN CONSTABLE: *Waterloo-Celebrations at East Bergholt*

91

Department of Sculpture

THE ITALIAN SCHOOL

1. ANDREA PISANO: *Virgin and Child*

1. The marble statuette *Virgin and Child* by the Tuscan master Andrea Pisano dates from between 1330–1336, when the master was working on the reliefs of the bronze doors of the Baptistry in Florence. The type of the head of the Madonna and the rhythmic folds of the drapery are similar to those seen in the reliefs. The statuette is a superb example of carved marble, the details being as delicate as those found in ivory carvings. Traces of the original gilding can still be seen. It was originally acquired by the Hungarian collector Miklós Jankovich.

2. The polychrome, medium-size terracotta statue representing the *Seated Madonna and Child* shows the influence of the famous fifteenth-century Florentine sculptor Lorenzo Ghiberti, who in his *Commentarii* records that he made sketches and models for the use of other masters. This statue, too, must have been executed after a model by Ghiberti, as its elongated proportions, the rhythm of the soft folds of the garments and the loving expression on the face all recall Ghiberti's work.

2. FLORENTINE MASTER (FOLLOWER OF GHIBERTI):
Seated Madonna and Child

3. AGOSTINO DI DUCCIO: *The Archangel Gabriel*

4. The medium-size terracotta relief, *Madonna with Child,* is the work of Michelozzo Michelozzi of Florence, who first studied under Lorenzo Ghiberti, and later worked with Donatello. This terracotta relief now in the Museum may date from 1430–1450. The type of the Madonna's head reveals the influence of Donatello, while the shaping and composition of the figure of the Child point to the influence of Ghiberti. Originally polychrome, there are still traces of blue paint on the Madonna's robes.

3. This somewhat less than life-size terracotta statue of the *Archangel Gabriel* still showing traces of the original paint, formed part of a group representing the Annunciation. Agostino di Duccio of Florence has in this work fused Florentine and Northern Italian influences to create an individual style of his own. His works in bas-relief are dominated by the beautiful undulating lines of the silhouette. This statue with its settled, restrained type of carving dates from the artist's second Perugian period from 1470–1480, presumably when he was working on the sculptures of the *Maestà della Volte* and the *Geraldini tomb.*

4. MICHELOZZO MICHELOZZI: *Madonna in a Shell-shaped Niche*

93

5. LEONARDO DA VINCI: *Equestrian Statue*

5. This small bronze study for an *Equestrian Statue* is a splendid example of Leonardo da Vinci's art. Throughout his life Leonardo constantly returned to the problems inherent in representing a man on a rearing horse. This is a theme found in many of his drawings and paintings. The conception is undoubtedly Leonardo's, but opinions differ as to the identity of the artist who carried it out. According to recent Hungarian research the model dates from Leonardo's last period, 1516–1519, in France, and the statuette has been identified as the "cavallo" which (according to Lomazzo's *Trattato*) was in the possession of Leone Leoni in 1584. The statuette, covered with artificial verd-antique, was purchased by the sculptor István Ferenczy in Rome sometime between 1818 and 1824.

6. In this small bronze statuette entitled *The Rape of Europa*, covered with artificial verd-antique, as in other small bronzes by Andrea Riccio (Briosco), the sculptor depicts a mythological subject through which he aims at the classical ideal of beauty. His sharp observation of nature endows his work with a lively quality, which earned him more praise from the humanists of Padua than they gave to his master, Bellano. This composition is a splendid example of the dramatic and powerfully expressive qualities of his work. Rage and indignation are expressed in the face and gestures of the daughter of the legendary king of Tyre, as she struggles to escape Zeus, who in the form of a bull, is carrying her away as his captive. The statuette dates from the master's mature period, in the early 1500s. It seems to be an individual piece, as no copies are known at present. It was formerly in the collection of István Ferenczy.

94

7. JACOPO SANSOVINO: *Madonna and Child*

7. Jacopo Sansovino (Tatti) was active in Florence, Rome and Venice. This *Madonna and Child* statuette is an early work, originating probably from 1515–1518 as a study for his *Madonna* for the Florentine Mercato Nuovo, later lost. The execution is technically very interesting, the moulded wax being applied on a wooden core, and the textile draperies covered with stucco. The gilding of the statue lends unity to the whole. It was after this composition that Andrea del Sarto painted his fresco of *Caritas* for the Chiostro dello Scalzo in Florence.

8. This small bronze representing the mythological story of Heracles and the many-headed Hydra is a lively example of the Baroque, arresting from every aspect. Iolaus is shown standing beside Heracles and applying the flame of a torch to burn down the monstrous heads. Hungarian scholars have recently attributed the work to Alessandro Algardi, thus extending our knowledge of the work of that eminent Roman sculptor of the seventeenth century. Boldly composed, this group representing *Heracles Struggling with the Hydra of Lerna* originates from the master's best period, and was the only example of Italian Baroque in the Ferenczy Collection.

6. ANDREA RICCIO: *The Rape of Europa*

8. ALESSANDRO ALGARDI: *Heracles Struggling with the Hydra of Lerna*

95

9. FLEMISH MASTER: *Madonna and Child*

THE GERMAN AND AUSTRIAN SCHOOLS

10. This painted limestone *Madonna and Child* is of the type known as *Schöne Madonnen*—Beautiful Madonnas. Smaller than life-size, it is a typical example of the International Gothic style. Ever since the exhibition *Die Parler und der Schöne Stil* in Cologne in 1978–1979, most experts on the period have dated it from 1420–1430. For many years it was considered to be an example of one of the earliest types of the "Beautiful Madonnas"; today it is classed as a late specimen of the type. The spatial structure and the plasticity of the drapery are less ambitious than in the best of the earlier examples of the type. It is very probable that it originated somewhere in south-east Germany.

THE NETHERLANDISH SCHOOL

9. This small alabaster sculpture of the *Madonna and Child* by a Flemish master dates from about 1440. Several features indicate that the sculptor was influenced by principal exponents of Netherlandish art at that time. A knowledge of Van Eyck's paintings is discernible in the Madonna's head and the style of the rich drapery. Though small, the statuette gives the impression of a sturdy figure; at the same time, the detail is most delicately elaborated.

10. SOUTH GERMAN MASTER: *Madonna and Child*

96

11. SOUTH TYROLESE MASTER: *Calvary Group*

11. This small *Calvary Group* of painted and gilt limewood by a South Tyrolese master dates from about 1430 and may once have adorned the baldachin of an altar, as did the related group above the altar of St Sigmund in Pustertal. The statuettes are popular examples of the late International Gothic style. The master may have come from the circle of the St Sigmund Master, to whom a great many works have been attributed. The figures of the Budapest group are not servile copies of those on the St Sigmund altar, they rather point to a master influenced by the Salzburg example of the international style.

12. The painted figure of *St John the Evangelist,* carved in oak, is the work of a Cologne master from the third quarter of the fifteenth century. Originally it formed part of a Calvary group, of which the statue of the Virgin is also in the Budapest Museum, while the figure of Christ is in Grosskönigsdorf near Cologne. The group may have stood under the triforium of one of the churches in Cologne. The elongation of the figure was still a characteristic of sculptures in the third quarter of the fifteenth century. Recent restoration has revealed the original green of the garment and the red of the mantle.

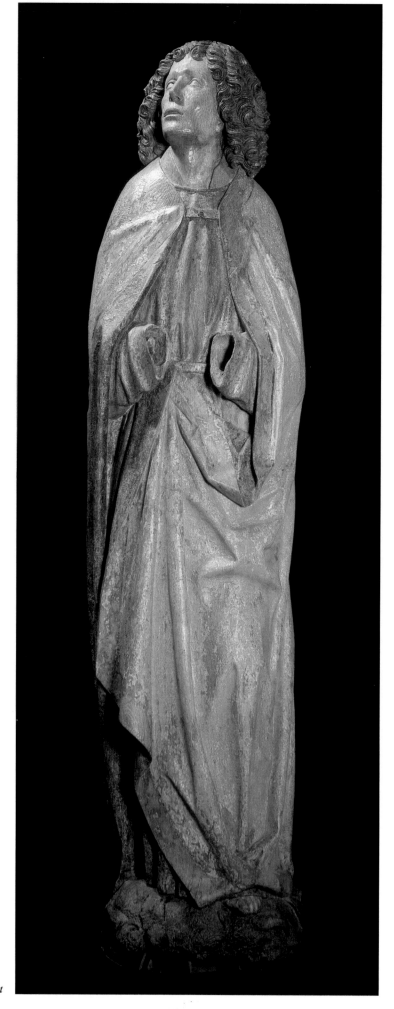

12. COLOGNE MASTER: *St John the Evangelist*

13. AUGSBURG MASTER: *Abundantia*

14. This is a splendid example of Alpine Baroque art. The figure of *Elisabeth,* less than life-size, was probably part of a Visitation group on a church altar made by Johann Meinrad Guggenbichler. Carved from yellow pine and covered with the original paint, it is thought to be the work of the German sculptor Johann Meinrad Guggenbichler, in whose art there is a harmonious fusion of the local mediaeval traditions with a dynamic representation of strong emotion.

13. This small bronze statuette representing *Abundantia* dates from between 1530–1540. Abundantia is represented touching her breast with her left hand; it is possible that originally she held a cornucopia in her right hand. Many variants of the bronze are known, mainly as fountain sculptures. The anonymous master is usually called the "Master of the Budapest Abundantia", and his works show the influence of North-Italian sculpture, but experts also point out the influence of classical statues of Venus. It used to belong to the Ferenczy Collection.

14. JOHANN MEINRAD GUGGENBICHLER: *Elisabeth*

15. GEORG RAPHAEL DONNER: *Atalanta*

16. GEORG RAPHAEL DONNER: *Meleager*

15–16. Georg Raphael Donner, a prominent exponent of Austrian Baroque, represented the slender figure of the Greek heroine *Atalanta* as she moves forward, thus creating spatial depth by means of the delicate movements of the right arm and the right foot. The beauty of the girl's classical head, as she turns towards Meleager, and the noble proportions of her body exemplify the harmonious effect achieved by Donner so markedly in contrast to the restlessness of Baroque art. This formal harmony is coupled with the painterly beauty of the light and shade effects which are so effective on the greyish surface of the lead. Atalanta was the heroine of the Greek myth which tells how she wounded the Calydonian boar and received as a prize from Meleager, who fell in love with her, the boar's skin and head. The athletic, muscular young man takes a light step forward; the head of the boar before his right foot refers to the Calydonian hunt. Both statuettes are individual pieces, no variants of them having been found so far. They were in the Bánffy Collection. Donner's works were very popular and numerous examples were acquired for Hungarian collections.

Department of Prints and Drawings

1. In 1503 Leonardo da Vinci was commissioned by the city of Florence to paint a fresco of the Battle of Anghiari for the Palazzo Vecchio. The fresco was never completed, but a reconstruction is possible. The red chalk *Warrior (The Red Head)* was created as the head of a mounted figure. It depicts the young warrior in profile, as he shouts his battle cry. The magic of the work rests on a delicate balance between the reproduction of reality and the classical ideal of beauty. It is a fine example of *sfumato,* which Leonardo made famous — the misty transitions of tone from light to dark.

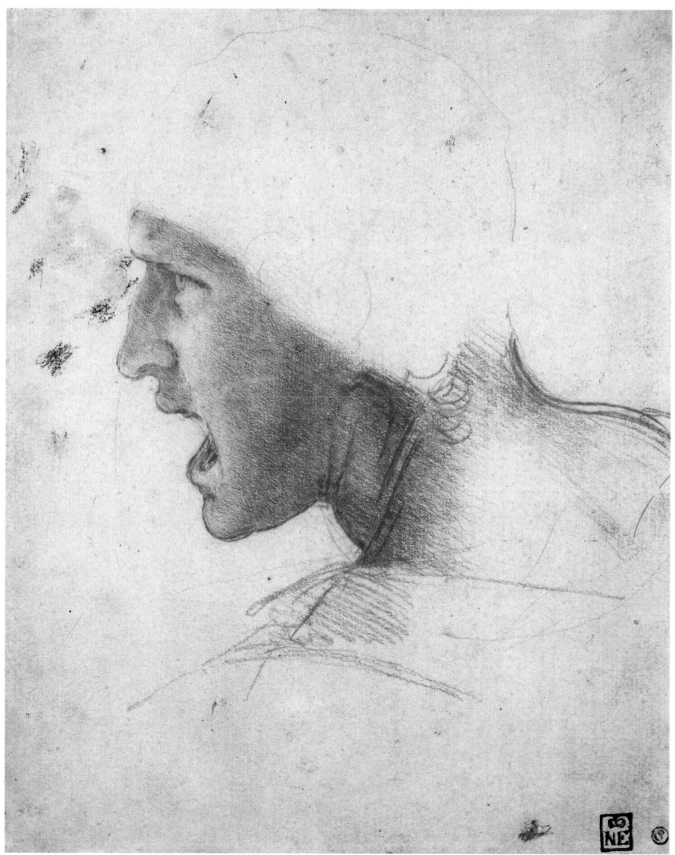

1. LEONARDO
DA VINCI: *Warrior*
("The Red Head")

2. VERONESE ARTIST: *The Manuscript Initial "M" with the Annunciation*

2. This miniature painting of the *Annunciation* within the manuscript initial "M", dating from between 1440–1450, was made by an excellent Veronese artist who may have worked under the influence of Stefano da Verona and Pisanello. The slender, delicately contoured figures painted in lively colours are so carefully finished that it would seem the artist found greater joy in figural painting than in the decorative details of the initial letter, which is in fact unfinished. The facial types and graceful gestures, refined in their simplicity, and the folds of the draperies, exhibit a mature, individual style. The artist has succeeded in blending the fifteenth-century skill in portraying figures and nature with the lyricism, and stylized formality of Gothic art.

3. Tintoretto's gift for creating dynamic compositions and expressing energy and movement, introduced a new spirit to sixteenth-century Venetian painting, already noted for its dexterous handling in the use of colour. His contribution is exemplified in this Budapest sheet with *drawings of a nude*. The figures were drawn from a bronze statuette thought to represent the wounded Philoctetes seen from different angles. The myth tells us that on his way to the Trojan War, the King of Thessaly suffered a snake-bite. His pain is expressed very precisely in two movements—the doubling over of the trunk and a giving way at the knee joints. Tintoretto made several studies of these reflex movements. He used small curved chalk-marks to convey the soft flexible contours of the figure, so that it seems to move, an impression enhanced by the representation of the muscles with faint outlines, delicate shading and white highlights.

3. JACOPO TINTORETTO: *Studies of a Model Statuette*

4. GIOVANNI DOMENICO TIEPOLO:
The Head of St James the Greater

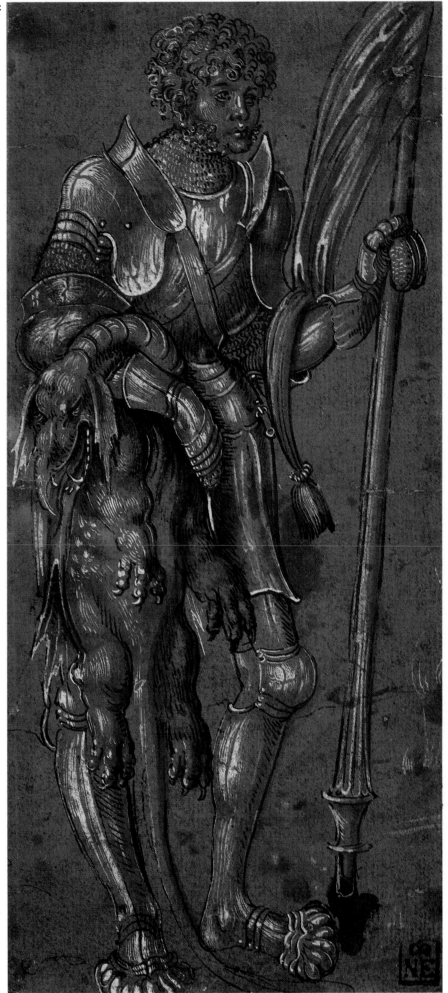

5. LUCAS CRANACH THE ELDER:
St George

4. Though at times believed to be a study made by Giambattista Tiepolo for his *St James the Greater Conquers the Moors,* now in Budapest, this drawing is now regarded as a copy of the Apostle's head made by the master's son, Giovanni Domenico. Giovanni Domenico, often considered the Hogarth of Italian art and a source of inspiration to Goya, found in his father's art a starting point for his own career, as may be seen from his many chalk drawings, including this representation of *St James the Greater.* By comparing it with his father's painting we recognize the son's different approach which is more realistic and matter-of-fact. Giovanni Battista Tiepolo's painting expresses the Apostle's sense of vocation, his almost trance-like ecstasy, while in the drawing of Giovanni Domenico the expression on the saint's face reflects a mood of youthful elation.

5. For his representation of St George, Lucas Cranach the Elder took his models from Dürer. This drawing of *St George* is related to a woodcut Cranach made in 1506. The saint's face is represented as serene rather than battle-hardened, in no way reminding us of his courageous deed; it is in fact very different from the strongly marked facial type in the woodcut. The shining suit of armour is depicted in minute detail and with loving care, shimmering decoratively against the dark background, giving liveliness to a composition otherwise archaic in its simplicity.

6. WOLF HUBER: *Studies of Trees with Castle*

7. Henry Fuseli (Johann Heinrich Füssli), a painter of Swiss extraction, developed an individual blend of neo-Classicism and Romanticism in his talented representations of supernatural elements and gloomy visions. The execution, however, shows a profound understanding of classical forms and pure, clear delineations. The figures in his visions were often modelled after his wife Sophia Ravlins. Her piquant face is to be seen in numerous portrait sketches, one of them being the watercolour *Portrait of a Woman* in Budapest. The rigid frontal posture, the huge round eyes and the hair arranged stiffly round the head like an extraneous headdress all contribute to the diabolic appearance of the sitter. The firmly outlined white figure depicted against a strongly contrasting dark grey background creates a harsh effect which is somewhat softened by the pale pinks introduced here and there in the dress.

6. Wolf Huber was a prominent artist of the Danube School which flourished in the first half of the sixteenth century. His art reflects his interest in nature, especially evident in his drawings, which constitute the major part of his *oeuvre*. The real subject of his *Studies of Trees with Castle* is the vitality of the plant kingdom, the richness of the vegetation; he introduces into his composition an abundance of plants, identical in detail, covering almost the entire sheet so that a spatial landscape is transformed into a decorative surface. The lack of atmosphere and sense of space turns the castle and the distant, snow-capped range of mountains into an improbable vision.

7. JOHANN HEINRICH FÜSSLI: *Portrait of a Woman*

104

8. JAN BRUEGHEL THE ELDER: *Winter Landscape with Travellers*

9. JACOB JORDAENS: *Family Scene*

8. This drawing depicting a *Winter Landscape with Travellers* by Jan Brueghel the Elder, a noted representative of Netherlandish landscape painting, may possibly date from around 1610–1620. The blue paper has been well chosen to harmonize with the cold colours of the winter landscape. The drawing represents a dream-like scene on the banks of a river where exhausted travellers are shown arriving with their horses and wagons. Their angular figures covered in warm garments cast hard shadows on the icy road. In the background is a misty view of the sailing boats and quayside buildings of a river port. In scale and colour this distant view of the port is very different from the scene in the foreground, a device used by the artist to enhance the sense of a spacious and extensive landscape.

9. The subjects chosen by Jacob Jordaens for his paintings are most earthly and the figures more plebeian than those seen in the works of Rubens and Van Dyck. Still, his paintings, mostly genre scenes, were characterized by a degree of vitality and pictorial quality similar to those of Rubens. The theme of his *Family Scene* is the handing over of the dowry in confirmation of a marriage settlement. The introduction of still-life objects such as the globe and the jugs, also the dog sleeping in the chair, helps to create an intimate atmosphere. The figures are contoured to create simple, angular forms. The pictorial quality is enhanced by the use of a combination of red chalk, brown and ash-blue ink and white body colour.

10. REMBRANDT HARMENSZ. VAN RIJN: *Dutch Peasant Cottage*

10. This is one of the finest of Rembrandt's early landscape drawings. It dates from 1636, a pen and brush drawing representing the porch and yard of a *Dutch Peasant Cottage*. The spontaneity of the composition seems to reflect the artist's moment of vision and inspiration as he perceived the magical effect of the afternoon sunlight on the homely scene. The side-wall of the outhouse and the covered porch are in deep shadow, while the patterned leaves of the vine shoots clinging to the roof are seen in full sunlight. The contrast between the broadly shaded patches of shadow and the delicate delineation of the dappled leaves adds to the picturesque quality of the composition.

11. Paulus van Vianen was a goldsmith to Emperor Rudolph II, and a pioneer in landscape drawing around 1600. Apart from numerous sensitively observed studies of landscapes, he made a number of attractive panoramas as well. One of them, *River Landscape with Rafts,* dates from 1601–1603, when Vianen was in Salzburg. There is a particular freshness in this representation of the swelling river and the rocky hillside shrouded in mist. He used pen strokes ranging from the hair-breadth lines of the detailed foliage to the bold strokes and light touches of the brush with which he indicates the majesty of the alpine landscape.

12. Jean-Antoine Watteau was the most outstanding exponent of the Rococo style famous for his "fêtes galantes", his figural compositions being both poetic and nostalgic. He represented his figures in silky dresses making refined and elegant gestures indicative of his familiarity with the callisthenics of the French ballet. He made many studies for these graceful figures, principally in red crayon. The female figures in this sheet he used for his paintings *Embarkation for the Island of Cythera* and *Walk on the Shore*. He modelled the women—one just about to rise from her sitting posture and the other moving forward—with soft, broken lines. The drapery is similarly indicated. Each of the three motifs is in fact complete in itself, yet together they give the impression of a single harmonious composition.

11. PAULUS VAN VIANEN: *River Landscape with Rafts* ▷

12. JEAN-ANTOINE WATTEAU: *Sketch Sheet* ▷

13. EUGÈNE DELACROIX: *Horse Frightened by Lightning*

13. This youthful masterpiece by Eugène Delacroix, entitled *Horse Frightened by Lightning,* is one of the most valuable works in the Museum, a fine example of the intense emotionalism of French Romanticism. The horse is represented in a state of frenzy, his terror expressed in the wildly tossing head and the rearing posture. The impression of swift movement is intensified by the virtually slurred representation of the flailing tail and mane. The cold light of the thunderbolt seems to bleach the chest of the rearing white horse depicted against stormy blue clouds, thus emphasizing the line of the head jerked back in the reflex of terror, the staring red eyes and the nostrils breathing fear.

14. The sketch *Barricade* by Édouard Manet depicts a street scene at the time of the Paris Commune, also represented in the painter's lithograph of the same title dating from 1871. In this composition the artist made use of one of his earlier lithographs depicting the execution of Emperor Maximilian of Mexico. In both works he expresses his political sympathies; in this picture he expresses his revulsion at the shooting down of communards in the street. The dramatic force of the work lies in its objectivity, the faint colours, the broken, sketchy brushwork and the dominant role assigned to the firing soldiers viewed from the rear but placed in the foreground of the composition.

15. Richard Parkes Bonington worked during his short but productive career in France, where his watercolours in particular were much praised. His first return to England in 1825 provided the inspiration for this watercolour of homeward bound sailing boats, *Off the English Coast,* of which there is a version in oil in the Wallace Collection in London. The watercolour, in delicate and harmonious colours, represents the typically Romantic theme of a stormy sea, yet it is rendered in a spirit of realism, and marked by a sensitive awareness of realistic detail. The theme is broadly conceived and freshly handled, but the artist nevertheless depicts convincingly the heaving waves and moist, windy atmosphere.

14. ÉDOUARD MANET:
Barricade

15. RICHARD PARKES
BONINGTON:
Off the English Coast

Department of Modern Art

1. FERDINAND GEORG WALDMÜLLER: *The Peep-show (Man with Stereoscope)*

1. Biedermeier painting flourished during the period of the Napoleonic wars and continued to find a market among the middle classes until 1848, the year of the revolution. This was the period when the middle and lower strata of society liked to see in their own homes pictures which echoed their own sentiments and ideals; they looked their owns of their own way of life that were basically realistic yet idealized in the handling. This demand was satisfied by the Biedermeier choice of subject, approach and size. The Museum of Fine Arts possesses an extensive and valuable collection of Austrian Biedermeier paintings. The most notable Viennese master of the style was Ferdinand Georg Waldmüller, whose *The Peep-show (Man with Stereoscope)* dates from 1847. An itinerant showman is exhibiting pictures to a group of villagers in an open barn and gesturing in a theatrical manner as he explains them. This conversation piece includes thirty figures posed in a manner reminiscent of the closing scenes of contemporary stage performances. There is also a moral issue to the scene—that the unspoiled peasant way of life exemplified by the simple pleasures enjoyed by healthy old country folk and their families is a better way of life than that of the enterprising traveller and his listless, weary daughter. The picture is of a type of painting intended to meet a specific social demand, using realistic means to create an idealized world.

2. EUGÈNE DELACROIX: *A Moroccan and His Horse*

3. JEAN-BAPTISTE CARPEAUX: *Spring*

2. This thoroughly Romantic painting by Eugène Delacroix dates from 1857. It includes a fine selection of Romantic elements—exotic, dark-skinned Arabs, the African landscape, the camp, the excitable dog yelping and rousing the horse to respond angrily. The whole composition of *A Moroccan and His Horse* conveys the atmosphere of unrest and agitation. The force of the wind is seen in the way the man struggles to hold the saddle-cloth and reach the restive thoroughbred whose mane is also held by the force of the gale. Dark clouds swirl across the sky and the eye finds rest only on the figures of the departing horseman and his companion in the background. The handling is light, the colours deep and fiery. We know from Delacroix's journal that he worked for a year on this splendid little canvas.

3. The French sculptor, Jean Baptiste Carpeaux, often worked in terracotta because it permits improvisation, speedy expression of ideas and feelings and is more immediately rewarding to the artist. On this bust of a young girl, the personification of Spring, the fluted neckline of her dress and the garland on her head retain a sense of the artist's swift-moving hands as he devised this means of framing the face and introducing the play of light and shade. The light modelling of the hair, the flowers and the dress is in perfect harmony with the carriage of the head, arrested momentarily but holding out the promise of an immediate further movement.

4. GUSTAVE
COURBET:
Spring at Fouras

5. EUGÈNE
BOUDIN:
Portrieux

4. There are in the Museum five pictures by Gustave Courbet, the founder of Realism in nineteenth-century European painting. They faithfully reflect the successive stages of his life as an artist and as a man. The *Spring at Fouras* dates from the period when Courbet's art was first recognized. In 1863 Courbet went to Fouras, partly for sea-bathing and partly to be with his friend Madame Borreau, represented in this picture sitting beside the fountain, posing for the artist who works in the shade of the trees. The human figures are almost unseen amidst the luxuriant vegetation and the dappled light penetrating the wood. Informal, full of light and colour, this is a particularly beautiful example of Courbet's art.

5. This painting represents a scene that is timeless in its tranquillity. The long shadows of late afternoon, already falling on the houses although the sun is still bright, will soon cover the sandy shore and reach the bare cliffs across the bay as the harnessed horses stand languidly on the hot sand. A group of women in frilly, ruffled dresses shade their faces under blue, green and yellow parasols, while men give a new coat of paint to a boat hauled up into the shade. The picture by Eugène Boudin, entitled *Portrieux* dates from 1874 and demonstrates that Eugène Boudin was already a great precursor of Impressionism. The scene is acutely observed and directly experienced, but the detail has been subtly fused into a single visual impression.

6. CAMILLE COROT: *Woman with Daisies*

6. Camille Corot owed his popularity principally to his landscapes—silvery grey paintings, lyrical in tone and reflecting the direct approach to nature of the Barbizon School. His figural works were appreciated only after his death. A fine example of the latter is the portrait *Woman with Daisies,* which he painted in his old age, around 1870. One feels it was painted after a model, but the artist has eschewed individuality in favour of idealization. The half-length figure of a woman, monumental in its effect, is depicted against a dark, neutral background. She wears a low-necked black dress with blue sleeves and a garland of daisies in her hair, which she holds with her left hand as it flows over her shoulder. The right hand is roughly sketched, as the picture was given, unfinished and unsigned, by the artist to his friend Gaspard Lacroix.

113

7. ÉDOUARD MANET:
Lady with Fan

8. CLAUDE MONET: *Fishing Boats*

7. Baudelaire was among those few who first appreciated the beauty of Édouard Manet's art. *Lady with Fan* is a relic of their friendship. In 1862 Manet painted a watercolour portrait of Jeanne Duval, who inspired *Les Fleurs du Mal*. This picture was modelled after the watercolour which can be seen in the Kunsthalle, Bremen. The créole actress shown seated on a dark green sofa was no longer young and the painter did not flatter her. Indeed, the youthful dress with blue stripes on a grey background, and the gossamer lace curtain behind her actually emphasize the hard features, the black-ringed eyes and matted black locks of the "Black Venus". The composition is dominated by the enormous tulle crinoline. It bears no relationship to the body beneath it yet the projecting leg is enough to confirm its reality. The painter used a bravura solution for the grey skirt, adding over-layers of blue, white, brown, red and other colours, even smearing the fresh paint with his fingers; in one place it is possible to see the trace marks of the five fingers.

8. Claude Monet, whose first master was Boudin, remained the most consistent adherent of open-air painting among his contemporaries. It was his work that gave to the movement its name, Impressionism. He was fascinated by the effects of light on colour and their consequent changes in the atmosphere, thus landscape became his principal subject. There are three of his landscapes in Budapest, *Fishing Boats* (1886) being the latest. He painted it in Étretat on the Normandy coast where, like many of his fellow-painters, he spent several summers. It was an area with many attractions, including the strange formations of the cliffs. The artist's handling of the shore and the water differ greatly. For the white-crested waves he applied broad, undulating brush-strokes and local colour, while he represented the shore with broken, scratchy brushwork with the rainbow colours so greatly favoured by the Impressionists. For the boats he used broad strokes to create a heavily impasted effect. His omission of the horizon was considered bold at the time.

9. CAMILLE PISSARRO:
The Pont-Neuf

9. During the course of a long and fertile career, Camille Pissarro changed his style of painting several times. The green landscape of La Varenne-de-Saint-Hilaire from around 1863 is still evenly illuminated by the summer sun with the local colours prevailing freely, an example of Impressionism in the making. *The Pont-Neuf* was painted in 1902, the year before the painter's death. Pedestrians, carriages and a crowded omnibus are seen making their way over the oldest bridge in Paris, his daily view from the window of his flat. This was the time when street scenes and glimpses of city life were becoming popular subjects for artists. It is a lively scene, vibrating with movement. The sunlight sparkles on the Seine and the whole canvas is suffused in light; it is a song of praise to the richness and variety of life. Pissarro dissolves the spectacle into tiny spots of colour which fuse into optical unity in the eye of the spectator.

13. GIOVANNI SEGANTINI: *The Angel of Life*

14. ARNOLD BÖCKLIN: *Spring Evening*

13. Giovanni Segantini, the child of a North Italian family of peasants, had received no tuition when he began to make realistic studies of the hill farmers and their way of life. Later, influenced by the work of the English Pre-Raphaelites, he developed a specific style of Nouveau symbolism. *The Angel of Life,* dating from 1894, represents a mother perched high up on the gnarled branch of a tree, holding a small child in her arms, as if removed from the world of everyday life. Smaller branches, fantastically looped, entwine her in their protective growth. The delicate carving of the frame, an organic part of the work, gives the impression of similarly entangled branches.

14. Arnold Böcklin, an influential Swiss German painter of the late nineteenth century, handled ancient traditions in a free manner. He created an individual mythology to represent the Pantheistic forces of nature and his own attitude to life. He painted *Spring Evening* in 1879 in Florence. The ancient Pan is seen blowing his pipe over the purplish-blue landscape, the young Dryads are posed in a rhythmic line with the straight and slanting trunks, and the enlarged, brightly-coloured flowers and sparkling stones stand out against the misty background, yet all are united in this harmonious composition. These dreaming mythical beings appear unaware of each other, yet like the musical reference, and especially the evening light brightening in the background, they add their own magic to the elegiac mood.

15. The Austrian Oskar Kokoschka, painted *Veronica's Veil* in 1911 in Vienna at a time when he was also engaged on several large religious compositions. It is one of the most important of his early works and in his autobiography he commented on the strange theme which it represents: "...that the reflection of a dying God might be imprinted on a kerchief is a visionary idea which could only be conceived by the religious painters of the Middle Ages." There is in fact a visionary quality in the tragic figure of the woman haloed by a mysterious light, watched by the enigmatic face of the moon, and holding the kerchief with the face of Christ as gently as if it were her child. It is a powerful creation, in which the spirit of German Gothic art is fused with an awareness of the psychology of mystic and imaginative experiences.

15. OSKAR KOKOSCHKA: *Veronica's Veil*

16. ÉTIENNE BÉOTHY: *Nuclear Form II*

16. A founding member of *Abstraction-Création,* Étienne Béothy, though Hungarian by birth, lived in Paris from 1927 onwards. There is a lyric quality as well as mathematical precision in his work. His *Nuclear Form,* dating from 1930, is monumental in effect though small in size. The eye finds pleasure in following the complicated waves of the continuous ribbon form, turning now outwards, now inwards, now again coiling in a spiral. Each aspect surprises us with new harmonies of outline, mass and rhythm. The aesthetic experience offered by technically perfect execution is enhanced by the rich colour of the polished mahogany.

Works in the Collections

Paintings

ALLODFER, HANS VON
The Liberation of Hungaria

ADRIAENSSEN, ALEXANDER
Still-life with Fish

AELST, WILLEM VAN
Still-life with Fruit

AERTSEN, PIETER
Market Scene

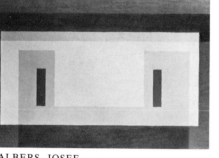

ALBERS, JOSEF
Light Grey Wall

ALBERT ALTAR, MASTER OF
Nativity

ALCIRA MASTER
Allegory

ALTDORFER, ALBRECHT
The Virgin and Child

ALTDORFER, ALBRECHT
Lovers

ALTOMONTE, MARTINO
The Young Man of Naim Raised

121

ARENT, ARENTSZ, VAN DER CABEL
Landscape with Hunters

AMERLING, FRIEDRICH VON
Portrait of Mrs Nákó née Berta Gyertyánffy

ANGUISCIOLA, SOPHONISBA
The Virgin and Child (Madonna del Latte)

ASSELYN, JAN
Italian Landscape

ASSERETO, GIOVACCHINO
The Mocking of Job

AVERCAMP, HENDRICK
Winter Scene with Skaters

BACCHIACCA (FRANCESCO UBERTINI)
St John the Baptist Preaching

BACKER, JACOB ADRIAENSZ.
Hearing

BALDOVINETTI, ALESSIO
The Calvary

BALDUNG GRIEN,
HANS
Mater Dolorosa

BALEN, HENDRICK VAN
Diana and Actaeon

BALEN, HENDRICK VAN
Allegory of Public Welfare

BARTOLOMMEO VENETO
Portrait of a Man

BAROCCI, FEDERICO (?)
The Annunciation with St Francis of Assisi

BARTOLOMMEO, DI GENTILE
Madonna Enthroned with Saints

BASAITI, MARCO
St Catherine of Alexandria

BASSANO, LEANDRO (?)
Portrait of an Old Man

BASSANO, GEROLAMO
Sleeping Shepherd

BASTIEN-LEPAGE, JULES
All Souls' Day

BAZZANI, GIUSEPPE
The Departure of the Prodigal Son

BELLUCCI, ANTONIO
Danae

BELLOTTO, BERNARDO
The Piazza della Signoria in Florence

BEMBO, GIOVANNI FRANCESCO
Portrait of Galeazzo Pallavicino

BENEDETTI, ANDRIES
Still-life with Fruit, Oysters and Crabs

BERCHEM, NICOLAES (PIETERSZ.)
Landscape with Resting Shepherds

123

BERNE CARNATION, MASTER OF THE
The Dance of Salome

ST BARTHOLOMEW ALTARPIECE,
MASTER OF *The Holy Family*

BEUCKELAER, JOACHIM
Market Scene

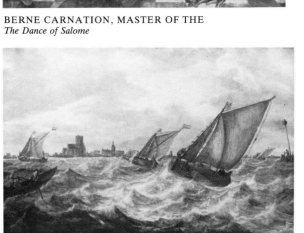

BEYEREN, ABRAHAM HENDRICKSZ. VAN
Rough Sea

BINOIT, PETER
Flowers in a Vase

BLES, HERRI MET DE
Rocky Landscape with Foundry

BOCCACCINO, BOCCACCIO
The Holy Family with St Jerome

BLOCKLANDT, ANTHONIE VAN
The Adoration of the Shepherds

BOILLY, LOUIS-LÉOPOLD
Visiting Grandfather

BOLTRAFFIO,
GIOVANNI ANTONIO
The Lodi Madonna

BONIFAZIO, VERONESE
Christ and the Woman Taken in Adultery

BONNARD, PIERRE
Mother and Child

BONNARD, PIERRE
The Luncheon

BORGOGNONE (AMBROGIO
DA FOSSANO) *The Lamentation*

BORGOGNONE
St Roch and St Louis of Toulouse

BORSSOM, ANTHONIE VAN
River-bank with a Lonely Horseman

BOTH, JAN
Woodland Scene

BOURDON, SÉBASTIEN
Bacchus and Ceres with Nymphs and Satyrs

BÖCKLIN, ARNOLD
The Centaur at the Smithy

BREU THE ELDER, JÖRG
The Raising of the Cross

BRONZINO, AGNOLO
Venus, Cupid and Jealousy

BROUWER, ADRIAEN
Peasants Smoking

BRUEGHEL THE ELDER, JAN
The Fall of Man

BRUEGHEL THE YOUNGER, PIETER
The Crucifixion

125

BRUEGHEL THE YOUNGER, PIETER
Village Fair

△

BRUSASORCI, FELICE
The Body of Christ with Angels

BRUYN THE ELDER, BARTHEL
Petrus von Clapis

BRUGGE
HOLY BLOOD ALTAR,
MASTER OF
Lucretia

BRUSSELS PAINTER
The Nativity

BUDAPEST MASTER
Pentaptych

BYE, HARMEN DE
Bust of a Woman

BYLERT, JAN VAN
The Calling of St Matthew

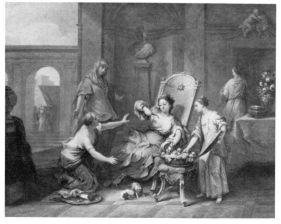

BYSS, JOHANN RUDOLF
The Death of Cleopatra

126

CAMPI, VINCENZO
Peasant Family at Meal

CANO, ALONSO
Noli me tangere

CANO, ALONSO *The Vision of
St John the Evangelist on the
Island of Patmos*

CARACCIOLO, GIOVANNI
BATTISTA *The Lamentation over Abel*

CARDUCHO, VICENTE
The Vision of St Francis

CARLI, RAFFAELE DE'
The Holy Family with an Angel

CARLONE, CARLO
The Deposition

CARPI, GIROLAMO DA
Christ and the Woman Taken in Adultery

CARPIONI, GIULIO
Iris in the Realm of Morpheus

CARREÑO DE MIRANDA, JUAN
St James the Greater Conqeuring the Moors

CASTELLO, VALERIO
St John the Baptist Preaching

CATENA, VINCENZO DI BIAGIO
*The Virgin and Child with St Francis, a Female
Saint and Donor*

CATENA, VINCENZO DI BIAGIO
The Holy Family with a Female Saint

CAXES, EUGENIO
The Adoration of the Magi

127

CECCARELLI, NADDO
The Virgin and Child

CELESTI, ANDREA
The Holy Family

CEREZO THE YOUNGER, MATEO
Ecce Homo

CHAGALL, MARC
Village in Blue

CHAMPAIGNE, PHILIPPE DE
Portrait of Henri Groulart

CHARDIN, JEAN-BAPTISTE SIMÉON
Still-life with Turkey

CHASSÉRIAU, THÉODORE
La Petra Camera

CIGNANI, CARLO
The Fall of Man

CIGOLI, LODOVICO CARDI DA
The Virgin and Child

CIPPER, GIACOMO FRANCESCO
Young Peasant Couple with Musicians

CLAESZ, PIETER
Still-life

CLERCK, HENDRICK DE
Rest on the Flight to Egypt

COCXIE, MICHIEL VAN
Portrait of Christina, Widow of the Duke of Lorraine

COLOMBEL, NICOLAS
Hagar and the Angel

CONSTABLE, JOHN
The Dam

COELLO, CLAUDIO
St Dominic

COELLO, CLAUDIO
The Holy Family

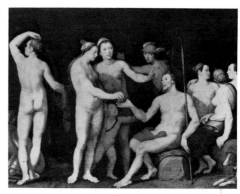

COQUES, GONZALES
A Family from Antwerp

CORNELIS VAN HAARLEM
The Golden Age (Bacchanalia)

CORNELIS VAN HAARLEM
The Judgement of Paris

COROT, JEAN-BAPTISTE CAMILLE
Italian Landscape

COROT, JEAN-BAPTISTE CAMILLE
Souvenir de Coubron

COSTA, LORENZO
The Holy Family with St Jerome and St Francis

COTER, COLYN DE
St John the Evangelist

COTER, COLYN DE
Mary Magdalene

COURBET, GUSTAVE
The Wrestlers

COURBET, GUSTAVE
Landscape with Pine Tree

129

COURBET, GUSTAVE
The Lake of Neuchâtel

COUTURE, THOMAS
Bird-catching

COZZARELLI, GUIDOCCIO
The Virgin and Child Enthroned with Saints

CRABETH, WOUTER PIETERSZ.
Company Playing Music

CRANACH THE ELDER, LUCAS
The Lamentation

CRANACH THE ELDER, LUCAS
The Angel Appearing to Joachim

CRANACH THE ELDER, LUCAS
Christ and the Adulteress

CRESPI, DANIELE
The Entombment of Christ

CUYP, AELBERT
Family Portrait by the Rhine

CUYP, BENJAMIN GERRITSZ.
The Angel at the Tomb of Christ

DAUBIGNY, CHARLES-FRANÇOIS
Landscape near Villerville

DELACROIX, EUGÈNE
Arabs Camping

DENIS, MAURICE
Maternal Bliss

DIAMANTE DI FEO
Virgin and Child Enthroned with Saints

DIOTISALVI, DI SPEME
Book Cover (Biccherna)

DIZIANI, GASPARE
The Adoration of the Magi

DOSSI, DOSSO
Madonna with Saints

DOU, GERARD
An Officer of the Leyden Civic Guara

DUGHET, GASPARD
Imaginary Landscape

DUJARDIN, KAREL
Tobias and the Angel

DYCK, SIR ANTHONY VAN
Portrait of a Married Couple

DOYEN, GABRIEL-FRANÇOIS
Juno and Aeolus

DYCK, SIR ANTHONY VAN
Portrait of a Man

EECKHOUT, GERBRANDT VAN DEN
A Family Group

EECKHOUT, GERBRANDT VAN DEN
Abraham and Melchizedek

131

GADDI, TADDEO
The Nativity

GADDI, TADDEO
The Deposition

GAINSBOROUGH, THOMAS
Charles Hotchkiss

GALLÉN-KALLELA, AKSELI
Young Faun

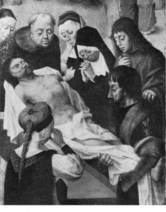

GAUGUIN, PAUL
Winter Landscape

GEERTGEN, TOT SINT JANS,
FOLLOWER OF *The Entombment*

GENTILESCHI, ARTEMISIA
Jael and Sisera

GHEZZI, GIUSEPPE
Pygmalion

GHIRLANDAIO, DOMENICO, FOLLOWER OF
St John the Evangelist on the Island of Patmos

GHIRLANDAIO, RIDOLFO
The Adoration of the Shepherds

GHISLANDI, FRA VITTORE
Portrait of a Young Painter

GIAMBONO, MICHELE
Virgin and Child Enthroned

GIAMPIETRINO (GIOVANNI PEDRINI)
*Virgin and Child with St Jerome and the
Archangel St Michael*

GIAQUINTO, CORRADO
The Allegory of Painting

GIORDANO, LUCA
The Flight into Egypt

GIORDANO, LUCA
Venus, Adonis and Cupid

GIORGIONE, AFTER
Self-portrait

GIOVANNI DI PAOLO
St Matthew with the Angel

GIULIO, ROMANO, FOLLOWER OF
Orion and Artemis

GOBIN, MICHEL
Boy Smoking a Pipe

GOYA Y LUCIENTES, FRANCISCO JOSÉ DE
The Knife-grinder (El Afilador)

GOVAERTS, ABRAHAM
Forest Scene

GOYA Y LUCIENTES, FRANCISCO JOSÉ DE
Portrait of the Marqués Caballero

GOYEN, JAN VAN
Rough Sea

GRAN, DANIEL
*St Elizabeth of Hungary
Distributing Alms*

GOYEN, JAN VAN
Landscape with Peasants

EL GRECO (DOMENIKOS THEOTOKOPOULOS)
The Disrobing of Christ (El Expolio)

135

EL GRECO (DOMENIKOS
THEOTOKOPOULOS)
The Annunciation

EL GRECO (DOMENIKOS
THEOTOKOPOULOS)
The Holy Family with St Elizabeth

EL GRECO (DOMENIKOS
THEOTOKOPOULOS)
St Andrew

GREUZE, JEAN-BAPTISTE
Portrait of a Girl

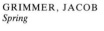

GRIMMER, JACOB
Spring

GRUND, NORBERT
Moses before the Burning Bush

GUARDI, FRANCESCO
Bridge at Dolo

GUARDI, GIOVANNI ANTONIO
Madonna with Saints

GUTTUSO, RENATO
Appropriating Land in Sicily

HACKERT, JACOB PHILIPP
River Landscape

HALS, DIRCK
A Merry Party

HALS, FRANS
The Painter Jan Asselyn

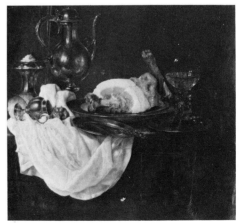

HEDA, WILLEM CLAESZ.
Still-life with Ham

136

HEEM, JAN DAVIDSZ. DE
Still-life with Oysters and Fruit

HEEMSKERCK, MAERTEN VAN
The Lamentation

HELST, BARTHOLOMEUS VAN DER
Admiral Gideon de Wildt

HEMESSEN, JAN DE
St Paul and St Barnabas Healing a Cripple at Lystra

HEMESSEN, JAN DE
Isaac Blessing Jacob

HERRERA THE ELDER, FRANCISCO DE
St Joseph with the Infant Jesus

HEYDEN, JAN VAN DER
Interior with Curios

HOGARTH, WILLIAM
Lady Thornhill

HOLBEIN THE ELDER, HANS
The Death of the Virgin

HOOCH, PIETER DE
Woman Reading a Letter

HOPPNER, JOHN
Mrs Swete

HUYSUM, JAN VAN
Flowers in a Vase

ISENBRANDT, ADRIAEN
*Crucifixion with St Andrew,
St Michael and St Francis*

137

JACOBELLO DEL FIORE
The Virgin and Child (Madonna dell'Umiltà)

JACOPO DEL CASENTINO
Virgin and Child Enthroned with Angels and Saints

JACOPO, DI CIONE
Madonna with Angels Playing Music

JACQUE, CHARLES-ÉMILE
In the Pasture

JANSSENS THE ELDER, ABRAHAM
Diana and Callisto

JONGH, LUDOLPH DE
Landscape with Resting Flock and Two Horsemen

JORDAENS, JACOB
The Peasant and the Satyr

JORDAENS, JACOB
Portrait of a Man

JUANES, JUAN DE
Christ with the Eucharist

KALF, WILLEM
Still-life with Fruit

KASTILIAN MASTER
*Presentation of the Virgin
in the Temple*

KAULBACH,
FRIEDRICH AUGUST
VON *Portrait of
Mrs Mihály Munkácsy*

KEYSER, THOMAS DE
Portrait of a Woman

KHANENKO ADORATION, MASTER OF THE
The Adoration of the Magi

KHNOPFF, FERNAND
Brook

138

KNÜPFER, NICOLAUS
Christ before Pilate

KOKOSCHKA, OSKAR
Poster Design for 'Der Sturm'

KUPETZKY, JOHANN
Man Playing the Shawm

KUPETZKY, JOHANN
The Artist and His Family

LAER, PIETER VAN
Landscape with Peasants Playing Morra

LA HIRE, LAURENT DE
Cornelia Rejecting the Crown of the Ptolemies

LA HIRE, LAURENT DE
Theseus and Aethra

LAIRESSE, GERARD DE
The Allegory of Constancy

LANGETTI, GIOVANNI BATTISTA
Joseph in Prison Interpreting Dreams

LASTMAN, PIETER
Tobias and the Angel with the Fish

LAZZARINI, GREGORIO
Faith, Hope and Charity

LE BRUN, CHARLES
The Apotheosis of Louis XIV

LEIBL, WILHELM
Pál Szinyei Merse

LELY, SIR PETER
Portrait of Frances Stuart

139

LENBACH, FRANZ VON
The Triumphal Arch of Titus in Rome

LIBALT, GOTTFRIED
Shot Fowl

LIBERALE DA VERONA
The Virgin and Child with an Angel

LIBERI, MARCO
Jupiter and Mnemosyne

LICINIO, BERNARDINO
Portrait of a Woman

LIEVENS, JAN
Portrait of a Girl

LISS, JOHANN
A Country Wedding Procession

LOIR, NICOLAS
Cleobis and Biton

LOO, JEAN-BAPTISTE VAN
Apollo and Daphne

LORENZETTI, AMBROGIO
Virgin and Child Enthroned

LORENZO
DA VITERBO
Christ Blessing

LORENZO, MONACO
Christ on the Cross

LOTTO, LORENZO
Virgin and Child with St Francis

LUINI, BERNARDINO
*Virgin and Child with St Elizabeth and the
Young St John the Baptist*

140

MAES, NICOLAS
Christ before Pilate

MAES, NICOLAS
Justus Criex

MARY MAGDALENE LEGEND,
MASTER OF THE
Christ in the House of Simon the Pharisee

MARY MAGDALENE LEGEND
MASTER OF THE *Queen Mary of Hungary*

MAGNASCO, ALESSANDRO
Friars at Lunch

MAGNELLI, ALBERTO
Embrace

MAKART, HANS
Nessus Carries off Deianeira

MAN, CORNELIS DE
The Chess Players

MANGLARD, ADRIEN
River Scene

MARCHESI DA COTIGNOLA,
GIROLAMO *The Lamentation*

MASTER OF
LIFE OF THE VIRGIN
The Virgin of Mercy

MARTÍNEZ, JUAN
Cushions

MARZIALE, MARCO
The Lamentation

MATEJKO, JAN ALOYSIUS
The Battle of Varna

141

MAULBERTSCH, FRANZ ANTON
Rebecca at the Well

MAULBERTSCH, FRANZ ANTON
The Apotheosis of St Stanislas

MATTEO DI GIOVANNI
The Apostle St Bartholomew

MAZZOLA BEDOLI, GIROLAMO
The Holy Family with St Francis

MAZZOLINO, LODOVICO
Christ before Pilate

MENGS, ANTON RAPHAEL
The Holy Family

MENZEL, ADOLF VON
Sermon in the Beech Grove near Kösen

MEYTENS, MARTIN VAN
Self-portrait

MICHELE DA VERONA
The Dead Christ with Angels

MIGNARD, PIERRE
Clio

MOLENAER, JAN MIENSE
A Merry Company before a Tavern

MIGNON, ABRAHAM
Flower-piece with Fish and a Birds' Nest

MOEYAERT, CLAES CORNELISZ.
Joseph Selling Wheat in Egypt

MOLENAER, JAN MIENSE
The Music Makers

MOMPER, JOOS DE
Divine Service in a Cave

MONET, CLAUDE
The Harbour at Trouville

MONET, CLAUDE
Apple-trees in Blossom

MONTAGNA, BARTOLOMMEO
Alfonso II, King of Naples, Gives Niccolò Orsini a Banner

MONTAGNANA, JACOPO DA
Pietà

MORETTO DA BRESCIA
St Roch with an Angel

MORETTO DA BRESCIA
A Martyr Saint

MORLAND, GEORGE
The Pigsty

MURA, FRANCESCO DE
The Virgin and Child

MURILLO, BARTOLOMÉ ESTÉBAN
The Flight into Egypt

MURILLO, BARTOLOMÉ ESTÉBAN
The Holy Family with the Young St John the Baptist

NALDINI, BATTISTA
The Three Graces

NALDINI, BATTISTA
The Crucifixion

NEER, AERT VAN DER
Moonlit Landscape

NERI DI BICCI
Madonna Enthroned

NETSCHER, CASPAR
The Presentation of a Locket

NEYN, PIETER DE
Sandy Path

NICCOLÒ DA FOLIGNO
St Bernardino of Siena

NICCOLÒ DI BUONACCORSO
The Annunciation

**NICCOLÒ DI SEGNA
DI BUONAVENTURA**
The Coronation of the Virgin

NUÑEZ DE VILLAVICENCIO, PEDRO
Spilt Apples

NORTH-ITALIAN PAINTER
Orsina de Grassi

NORTH-ITALIAN PAINTER
Portrait of Vittoria Farnese

OCHTERVELT, JACOB
A Dutch Family

OGGIONO, MARCO D'
Angel with Censer

OPIE, JOHN
Portrait of a Woman

ORRENTE, PEDRO
The Supper at Emmaus

OSTADE, ADRIAEN VAN
Peasant Family

OSTADE, ADRIAEN VAN
Pen Sharpener

OSTADE, ISAACK VAN
Pig-killing

OVENS, JÜRGEN
A Mother and Her Children

PACHER, FRIEDRICH
Christ in Limbo

PALMA GIOVANE
The Dead Christ with Two Angels

PALMA VECCHIO
Bust of a Youth

PALMA VECCHIO
Bust of a Girl

PENNACCHI, GIROLAMO
Kitchen Still-life

PELLEGRINI, GIOVANNI
ANTONIO *Christ Healing the
Man Stricken with Palsy*

PAUDISS, CHRISTOPH
Virgin and Child

145

PEREDA, ANTONIO
St Anthony of Padua Worshipping the Infant Christ

PETTENKOFEN, AUGUST VON
Fair at Szolnok

PIAZZA DA LODI, MARTINO
*Virgin and Child with the Young
St John the Baptist*

PIERO DI COSIMO
Christ on the Cross

PIETRO DA MESSINA (PIETRO
DE SALIBA) *Christ at the Column*

PINO, MARCO DAL
Ecce Homo

PIOMBO, SEBASTIANO DEL
Portrait of a Girl

PIOMBO, SEBASTIANO DEL
Christ Bearing the Cross

PISSARRO, CAMILLE
La Varenne-de-St-Hilaire

PITTONI, GIOVANNI BATTISTA
St Elizabeth of Hungary Distributing Alms

PITTONI, GIOVANNI BATTISTA
The Nativity

POELENBURGH, CORNELIS VAN
*The Children of Elector Palatine Frederic V,
King of Bohemia*

PORCELLIS, JAN
Stormy Sea

146

PORDENONE, GIOVANNI
ANTONIO DA
St Luke

POTTER, PAULUS
Landscape with a Shepherd and a Shepherdess

POUSSIN, NICOLAS
The Rest on the Flight into Egypt

PREVITALI, ANDREA
The Virgin and Child

PYNACKER, ADAM
Rocky Landscape with Waterfall

QUESNEL, AUGUSTIN
Woman Playing the Guitar

REMBRANDT, HARMENSZ.
VAN RIJN *The Old Rabbi*

REMBRANDT, HARMENSZ. VAN RIJN
The Slaughtered Ox

REMBRANDT, HARMENSZ. VAN RIJN and DOU, GERARD
The Parable of the Hidden Treasure

REMBRANDT, HARMENSZ. VAN RIJ
FOLLOWER OF *Portrait of a Woman*

RENI, GUIDO
David and Abigail

RENOIR, AUGUSTE
Portrait of a Girl

RIBOT, THÉODULE
Still-life

147

RICCI, SEBASTIANO
Moses Defending the Daughters of Jethro

RICCI, SEBASTIANO
The Assumption

RICCI, SEBASTIANO
Venus and the Satyr

RIGAUD, HYACINTHE
Cardinal Fleury

ROCCA, MICHELE
Samson and Delilah

ROMAKO, ANTON
August Wassermann

ROMANINO, GIROLAMO
Portrait of a Man

ROOS, JOHANN HEINRICH
A Shepherd and His Family at the Well

ROSA, FRANCESCO DE
Moses Brings Forth Water out of the Rock

ROSA, SALVATOR
Seaport with Ruins

ROSSELLI, MATTEO
The Allegory of Fidelity

ROTARI, PIETRO
Girl with Distaff

RUBENS, SIR PETER PAUL
Study of a Man's Head

RUISDAEL, JACOB VAN
Forest Lake

148

RUYSDAEL, SALOMON VAN
Riverscape with Ferry

RUYSDAEL, SALOMON VAN
After the Rain

RUYSDAEL, SALOMON VAN
Battle Scene with Cavalry

RUYSDAEL, SALOMON VAN
Inn with a Maypole

RYCKAERT III, DAVID
A Merry Company

RYCKAERT III, DAVID
The Adoration of the Shepherds

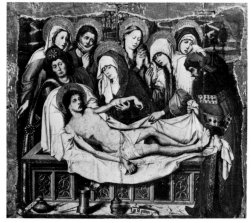

SÁNCHEZ, PEDRO
The Entombment

SANO DI PIETRO (ANSANO DI PIETRO DI MENCIO)
The Dance of Salome

SANTI, GIOVANNI, SCHOOL OF
Madonna Enthroned with Saints

SAVERY, ROELANDT JACOBSZ.
Landscape with Lion Lacerating a Cow

SCARSELLA, IPPOLITO
(LO SCARSELLINO)
The Mystic Marriage of St Catherine

SCHMIDT, MARTIN JOHANN
The Judgement of Solomon

149

SCHÖNFELD, JOHANN
HEINRICH *Aeneas and Anchises*

SELLAIO, JACOPO DEL
Esther before Ahasuerus

SELLAIO, JACOPO DEL
St John the Baptist

SEYBOLD, CHRISTIAN
Laughing Man with Black Pudding

SEVERINI, GINO
Portrait of the Artist's Wife

SIBERECHTS, JAN
The Ford

SIGNORELLI, LUCA,
WORKSHOP OF *Tiberius Gracchus*

SHISHKHIN, IVAN IVANOVICH
Woodland Scene

SITTOW, MICHEL
The Virgin and Child

SLEVOGT, MAX
Still-life with Flowers

SODOMA (GIOVANNI ANTONIO BAZZI)
The Scourging of Christ

SODOMA (GIOVANNI ANTONIO
BAZZI) *The Death of Lucretia*

SOLIMENA, FRANCESCO
The Martyrdom of St Placidus and Flavia

SPANZOTTI, GIOVANNI MARTINO
Pietà

150

SPRANGER, BARTHOLOMÄUS
Diana

STEEN, JAN
Courtesan

STELLA, JACQUES
The Betrothal of the Virgin

STEVENS, ALFRED
Woman Playing the Harp

STROZZI, BERNARDO
The Annunciation

STROZZI, BERNARDO
The Annunciation

STUCK, FRANZ VON
Spring

TADDEO DI BARTOLO
Madonna dell'Umiltà

TEMPEL, ABRAHAM VAN DEN
Portrait of a Married Couple

TENIERS THE YOUNGER, DAVID
The Barber-surgeon's Shop

TENIERS THE YOUNGER, DAVID
A Game of Tric-trac

TERBRUGGHEN, HENDRICK, CIRCLE OF
The Calling of St Matthew

TIEPOLO, GIOVANNI BATTISTA
The Virgin with Six Saints

151

TIEPOLO, GIOVANNI DOMENICO
The Rest on the Flight into Egypt

TINTORETTO (JACOPO ROBUSTI)
The Supper at Emmaus

TINTORETTO (JACOPO ROBUSTI)
Portrait of a Young Woman

TITIAN (TIZIANO VECELLIO)
Portrait of Cardinal Pietro Bembo

TUSCAN MASTER
Christ on the Cross

TOULOUSE-LAUTREC, HENRI DE
Ces Dames

TOURNIÈRES, ROBERT
Count Ferdinand Adolf von Plettenberg and His Family

TRECK, JAN JANSZ.
Still-life with Pewter Jug

TREVISANI, FRANCESCO
Lucretia

TRISTÁN, LUIS
The Adoration of the Magi

TROYON, CONSTANTIN
Cowherd

UHDE, FRITZ VON
The Sermon on the Mount

152

UTRILLO, MAURICE
The Street

UMBRIAN PAINTER
Allegorical Female Figures (Strength, Justice and Activity)

VACCARO, ANDREA
St Sebastian and the Holy Woman

VANNI, FRANCESCO
The Holy Family

VALCKENBROCH, FREDERICK VAN
Pilgrims Outside a Forest Chapel

VASARELY,
VICTOR
Marsan

VEERENDAEL, NICOLAES VAN
The Bust of the Virgin in a Garland

VELÁZQUEZ, DIEGO RODRÍGUEZ
DE SILVA Y, WORKSHOP OF
The Infanta Margaret Theresa

VELDE THE YOUNGER, WILLEM VAN DE
Warships on a Calm Sea

VERMEER THE ELDER, JAN
View of Haarlem from the Overveen Dunes

VERNET, JOSEPH
Landscape with Castle Ruins

153

VERONESE, PAOLO
The Crucifixion

VERSPRONCK, JAN
CORNELISZ.
Portrait of a Man

VICTORS, JAN
Abraham Sends Hagar Away

VIVARINI, ALVISE AND WORKSHOP
*The Virgin and Child with St John the Baptist
and St Jerome*

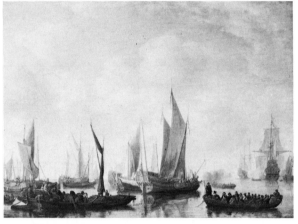

VLIEGER, SIMON DE
Ships on a Calm Sea

VLIEGER, SIMON DE
Landscape with River and Trees

VLIEGER, SIMON DE
Hunters at the Well

VOS, CORNELIS DE
A Family Portrait

VOUET, SIMON, WORKSHOP OF
Sleeping Venus

VRANCX, SEBASTIAN
Banquet in a Garden

WEENIX, JAN BAPTIST
The Ruins of the Temple of Vespasian in Rome

WERFF, ADRIAEN VAN DER
Susanna in Her Bath

WINKLER EPITAPH,
MASTER OF THE
The Martyrdom of St John the Evangelist

WITTE, EMANUEL DE
Interior of the Oude Kerk in Amsterdam

WOENSAM, ANTON
The Crucifixion

WOU, CLAES CLAESZ.
Rough Sea with Three Ships

WOUWERMAN, PHILIPS
The Riding School

WTEWAEL, JOACHIM ANTHONISZ.
The Judgement of Paris

WYCK, THOMAS
Italian Port

WYNANTS, JAN
Road by a Wood

ZAIS, GIUSEPPE
Landscape with River

ZELOTTI, GIAMBATTISTA
Allegorical Figure: Strength

ZOFFANY, JOHN
David Garrick and Susannah Maria Cibber on Stage

ZORN, ANDERS
Mother and Child

ZUCCARELLI, FRANCESCO
Landscape with Bridge

ZURBARÁN, FRANCISCO DE
The Holy Family

155

Drawings

ALT, RUDOLF VON
View of Pest-Buda with the Royal Castle

ALTDORFER, ALBRECHT
View of Sarmingstein

BALDUNG GRIEN, HANS
Christ with the Instruments of His Sufferings

BERNARD, PIERRE
Portrait of a Young Man

BLOEMAERT, ABRAHAM
Hunter with Dogs

BOLOGNINI CHAPEL, MASTER OF
Hunting Adventure

BURGKMAIR, HANS
Thetis Takes Achilles to the Island of Scyros

BURRINI, GIOVANNI
ANTONIO *Study for the Portrait of Beatus Tommaso Abruzze*

CARRACCI, LODOVICO
Study of a Nude

CÉZANNE, PAUL
Self-portrait

CLAUDE LORRAIN (CLAUDE GELLÉE)
Landscape (Stag Hunt)

CORREGGIO
(ANTONIO ALLEGRI)
The Virgin

CRESPI, DANIELE
St Cecilia

156

CUYP, AELBERT
Landscape with Sheep

DAUMIER, HONORÉ
Circus Parade

DIZIANI, GASPARE
Fighting Knights

DÜRER, ALBRECHT
Virgin and Child with St Anne

FRAGONARD, JEAN-HONORÉ
Cottage by the Forest

FÜGER, FRIEDRICH HEINRICH
The Twelve-year-old Christ in the Temple

GHEYN, JACQUES DE
Hippocrates and Democritus

GOGH, VINCENT VAN
The Nuenen Garden in Winter

GOLTZIUS, HENDRIK
Prophet

GUERCINO (GIOVANNI FRANCESCO BARBIERI)
Landscape

HUBER, WOLF
Brook with Willows

HUYSUM, JAN VAN
Still-life with Fruit

157

COLOGNE MASTER
St Margaret

KRIEHUBER, JOSEF
Portrait of a Man

LEONARDO DA VINCI
Heads of Warriors

LESUEUR, EUSTACHE
Juno

MARATTI, CARLO
Hera Tells Aeolus to Destroy the Trojan Fleet

MARÉES, HANS VON
Sketches for the Picture 'Idylls'

MAULBERTSCH, FRANZ ANTON
Young Man in Plumed Hat

MENZEL, ADOLF VON
Study Sheet

MILLET, JEAN-FRANÇOIS
Maternal Cares

ORLEY, BAREND VAN
Sharing the Game

OSTADE, ADRIAEN VAN
Dutch Peasant Family

158

PARMIGIANINO (FRANCESCO MAZZOLA)
Shepherd and Shepherdess

RAPHAEL (RAFFAELLO SANTI)
Female Nude (Psyche)

REMBRANDT HARMENSZ. VAN RIJN
Woman with Weeping Child and Dog

REMBRANDT HARMENSZ. VAN RIJN
Saskia

RENI, GUIDO
Sketch for 'The Crucifixion of St Peter'

RENOIR, AUGUSTE
After a Bath

RODIN, AUGUSTE
Sketch of Madame Séverine

ROSSETTI, DANTE GABRIEL
Study of a Head

SACCHETTI, LORENZO
Antique Ruins (set design)

159

BÉOTHY, Étienne
Heves, 1897—Paris, 1961
Nuclear Form II* (p. 120)
wood, 30 cm
signed and dated 1950

BERCHEM,
Nicolaes Pietersz.
Haarlem, 1620—
Amsterdam, 1683
Landscape with Resting
Shepherds
oil on panel,
46.8×56 cm
signed and dated, 1646

BERNARD, Pierre
active 1750–1800 (?)
Portrait of a Young Man
pastel on paper, 50×40 cm
signed and dated 1763

BERNE CARNATION,
Master of
late 15th century
The Dance of Salome
oil on panel,
102.5×123 cm
c. 1500

ST BARTHOLOMEW
ALTARPIECE, Master of
the
active in Cologne,
1470–1510
The Holy Family
oil on panel,
30.5×23 cm
1480s

BEUCKELAER, Joachim
Antwerp, *c.* 1535–1574
Market Scene
oil on panel,
113.5×81.5 cm
signed, late work

BEYEREN,
Abraham Hendricksz. van
The Hague, 1620/21—
Overschie, 1690
Rough Sea
oil on canvas,
69.8×112 cm
signed

BINOIT, Peter
active in Frankfurt
am Main, 1611–1624
Flowers in a Vase
oil on copper,
38.2×28.5 cm
signed and dated 1613

BLANCHARD, Jacques
Paris, 1600–1638
St Jerome* (p. 57)
oil on canvas,
145.5×116 cm
signed and dated 1632

BLES, Herri Met de
Bouvignes/Dinant, *c.*
1510—Antwerp. *c.* 1550
Rocky Landscape with
Foundry
oil on panel,
48.5×69 cm
signed

BLOCKLANDT,
Anthonie van

Montfoort, 1532—
Utrecht, 1583
The Adoration of the
Shepherds
oil on panel,
72×96 cm
signed, before 1562

BLOEMAERT, Abraham
Dordrecht, 1564—
Utrecht, 1651
Hunter with Dogs
wash, pen and ink,
9.3×15 cm
early 1610s

BOCCACCINO, Boccaccio
Ferrara, *c.* 1467—
Cremona, 1525
The Holy Family with
St Jerome
oil on panel,
148.7×108 cm
mature period

BOCCATI, Giovanni
Camerino, *c.* 1420—
after 1480
Virgin and Child Enthroned
with Four Saints and
Angels* (p. 32)
tempera on panel,
186.5×162 cm
22×217 cm (frieze)
diam. 19 cm (locket)
dated 1473

BOILLY, Louis-Léopold
Ort La Bassée, 1761—
Paris, 1845
Visiting Grandfather
oil on panel,
24.7×32.5 cm

BOLOGNINI CHAPEL,
Master of
Hunting Adventure
brush, pen and ink,
14.8×18.2 cm
c. 1400

BOLTRAFFIO,
Giovanni Antonio
Milan, 1467–1516
The Virgin and Child*
(p. 36)
oil on panel,
83×63.5 cm
late 15th century
The Lodi Madonna
oil on panel,
196×147.5 cm
after 1508

BONIFAZIO, Veronese
(Bonifazio de' Pitati)
Verona, 1487—Venice, 1553
Christ and the Woman
Taken in Adultery
oil on canvas,
163×202 cm
c. 1550 (with inscription)

BONINGTON,
Richard Parkes
Arnold, 1801—London,
1828
Off the English Coast*
(p. 109)
watercolour,
14.1×23.1 cm
signed and dated, 1825

BONNARD, Pierre
Fontenay-aux-Roses,
1867—Le Cannet, 1947
Mother and Child
oil on panel, 33×42 cm
signed and dated, 1894
The Luncheon
oil on canvas,
53.5×61 cm
signed, *c.* 1899

BORGOGNONE
(Ambrogio da Fossano)
Fossano or Milan, *c.*
1450—Milan, after 1522
The Lamentation
oil on panel,
64.7×49.3 cm
St Roch and St Louis
of Toulouse
oil on panel,
88×63.5 cm

BORSSOM, Anthonie van
Amsterdam, *c.* 1629–1677
River-bank with a Lonely
Horseman
oil on canvas,
55.5×72 cm
signed

BOTH, Jan
Utrecht, *c.* 1615 or
1622–1652
Woodland Scene
oil on canvas,
111×141 cm

BOUDIN, Eugène
Honfleur, 1824—
Paris, 1898
Portrieux* (p. 112)
oil on canvas,
54.3×89.3 cm
signed and dated, 1874

BOURDON, Sébastien
Montpellier, 1616—
Paris, 1671
Bacchus and Ceres with
Nymphs and Satyrs
oil on canvas,
51×77.5 cm

BÖCKLIN, Arnold
Basle, 1827—
S. Domenico, 1901
Spring Evening*
(p. 118)
oil on panel,
67.4×129.5 cm
signed, 1879
The Centaur at the Smithy
oil on panel, 80×100 cm
signed, 1888

BREU THE ELDER, Jörg
Augsburg, *c.* 1475–1537
The Raising of the Cross
oil on panel, 87×63 cm
signed and dated, 1524

BRONZINO, Agnolo
Florence, 1503–1572
The Adoration of the
Shepherds* (p. 47)
oil on panel,
65.3×46.7 cm
signed, late 1530s
Venus, Cupid and Jealousy
oil on panel,
192×142 cm
signed, mid-1540s

BROUWER, Adriaen
Oudenaerde, 1605/6—
Antwerp, 1638
Peasants Smoking
oil on panel,
40.7×39.3 cm

BRUEGEL THE ELDER,
Pieter ('Peasant Bruegel')
Groote-Brogel, *c.* 1522—
Brussels, 1569
St John the Baptist
Preaching*
(p. 64)
oil on panel,
95×160.5 cm
signed and dated, 1566

BRUEGHEL THE
ELDER, Jan
('Velvet Brueghel')
Brussels, 1568—
Antwerp, 1625
The Fall of Man
oil on panel,
52×83.5 cm
signed
Winter Landscape with
Travellers* (p. 105)
brush drawing,
13.6×21.6 cm
1610s

BRUEGHEL THE
YOUNGER, Pieter
('Hell Brueghel')
Brussels, 1564—
Antwerp, 1637/38
The Crucifixion
oil on panel, 82×123 cm
signed and dated, 1617
Village Fair
oil on panel,
114×161 cm

BRUSASORCI, Felice
Verona, *c.* 1539–1605
The Body of Christ with
Angels
slate, 41×47 cm

BRUYN THE ELDER,
Barthel
Wesel, 1493—
Cologne, 1555
Petrus von Clapis
oil on panel,
41×32.5 cm (incl. frame)
c. 1530

BRUGGE HOLY BLOOD
ALTAR, Master of
active *c.* 1520
Lucretia
oil on panel,
65×48.5 cm
c. 1520

BRUSSELS Painter
active *c.* 1520
The Nativity
oil on panel,
55.5×75 cm

BUDAPEST Master
active in Castile,
c. 1500
Pentaptych
transferred from panel to
canvas, 85×67.3 cm
75.5×44 cm
71×44 cm
c. 1500

BURGKMAIR, Hans
Augsburg, 1473–1531
Thetis Takes Achilles to
the Island of Scyros
pen and ink and brush
drawing, 20.5×15 cm
1518

BURRINI,
Giovanni Antonio
Bologna, 1656—1727
Study for the Portrait of
Beatus Tommaso Abruzze
pastel, 37.6×28.8 cm
1687

BUYTEWECH,
Willem Pietersz.
Rotterdam, 1591/2–1624
A Merry Company* (p. 71)
oil on canvas,
72.6×65.4 cm
c. 1620

BYE, Harmen de
1601/2–1670
Bust of a Woman
oil on canvas,
79.4×65.6 cm
signed and dated 1653

BYLERT, Jan van
Utrecht, 1598–1671
The Calling of St Matthew
oil on canvas,
128.3×200 cm

BYSS, Johann Rudolf
Solothurn, 1660—
Würzburg, 1738
The Death of Cleopatra
oil on panel,
30.7×40.2 cm
signed

CAMPI, Vincenzo
Cremona, 1536–1591
Peasant Family at Meal
oil on canvas, 92×78 cm

CANALETTO: see
BELLOTTO

CANO, Alonso
Granada, 1601–1667
Portrait of the Infante
Don Baltasar Carlos* (p. 88)
oil on canvas,
144×109.3 cm
c. 1634–1635
Noli me tangere
oil on canvas,
141.5×109.5 cm
signed, 1646–1652
The Vision of St John the
Evangelist on the Island of
Patmos
oil on canvas,
218×153 cm

CARACCIOLO,
Giovanni Battista
(Il Battistello)
Naples, *c.* 1570–1637
The Lamentation over Abel
oil on canvas,
193.5×146.4 cm

CARDI: see CIGOLI

CARDUCHO, Vicente
(Vicente Carducci)

Florence, 1578—
Madrid, 1638
The Vision of St Francis
oil on canvas,
246×173 cm
signed and dated 1631

**CARLI, Raffaele de'
(Raffaellino del Garbo)**
c. 1470–*c.* 1524 or later
*The Holy Family with
an Angel*
oil on panel,
diam. 102 cm
late work

CARLONE, Carlo
Scaria/Como, 1686–1775
The Deposition
oil on canvas,
79×46.5 cm
c. 1731

CARPEAUX, Jean-Baptiste
Valenciennes, 1827—
Courbevoie, 1875
*Spring** (p. 111)
terracotta, 53.7 cm
signed and dated 1874

CARPI, Girolamo da
Ferrara, 1501–1556
*Christ and the Woman
Taken in Adultery*
oil on panel, 55×44 cm

CARPIONI, Giulio
Venice, 1613—
Vicenza, 1679
*Iris in the Realm
of Morpheus*
oil on canvas,
137×148 cm

CARRACCI, Annibale
Bologna, 1560—
Rome, 1609
*Christ and the Woman
of Samaria**
(p. 49)
oil on canvas,
76.5×63.5 cm
c. 1590

CARRACCI, Lodovico
Bologna, 1555–1619
Study of a Nude
pastel, 24.6×23.8 cm
1604–1605

**CARREÑO DE
MIRANDA,
Juan**
Avilés, 1614—
Madrid, 1685
*St James the Greater
Conquering the Moors*
oil on canvas,
231×168 cm
signed and dated 1660

CASTELLO, Valerio
Genoa, 1625–1659
*St John the Baptist
Preaching*
oil on canvas,
166×215.5 cm

**CATENA, Vincenzo
di Biagio**
Venice (?), *c.* 1470–1531
The Virgin and Child with

*St Francis, a Female Saint
and Donor*
oil on panel,
64.7×92 cm
early 16th century
*The Holy Family with
a Female Saint*
oil on panel,
66×96.2 cm
signed, early 16th century

CAVALLINO, Bernardo
Naples, 1616—Naples (?),
c. 1656
*Joachim and Anne
at the Golden Gate**
(p. 53)
oil on canvas,
229×178.5 cm
c. 1640

**CAXES, Eugenio
(Eugenio Cajes)**
Madrid, 1577–1642
The Adoration of the Magi
oil on canvas,
183×186.5 cm

CECCARELLI, Naddo
active in Siena,
mid-14th century
The Virgin and Child
tempera on panel,
29.6×19.4 cm

CELESTI, Andrea
Venice, 1637—
Toscolano, 1712
The Holy Family
oil on canvas,
144×117 cm

**CEREZO THE
YOUNGER, Mateo**
Burgos, 1635—
Madrid, 1685
Ecce Homo
oil on canvas, 98×75 cm
signed

CÉZANNE, Paul
Aix-en-Provence,
1839–1906
*The Sideboard** (p. 117)
oil on canvas,
65×81 cm
1873–1877
Self-portrait
pencil, 30×25 cm
c. 1880

CHAGALL, Marc
Vitebsk, 1887—
Saint-Paul de Vence, 1985
Village in Blue
gouache on paper,
57.5×67 cm
signed, 1968

**CHAMPAIGNE,
Philippe de**
Brussels, 1602—
Paris, 1674
Portrait of Henri Groulart
oil on canvas,
92.5×75.5 cm
signed and dated 1654

**CHARDIN,
Jean-Baptiste Siméon**
Paris, 1699–1779
Still-life with Turkey

oil on canvas,
96×123 cm
signed

**CHASSÉRIAU,
Théodore**
Samana, 1819—
Paris, 1856
La Petra Camera
oil on panel,
32.2×23.4 cm
signed and dated 1832

**CHRISTUS, Petrus
(Petrus Cristus)**
Bearle *c.* 1420—Bruges,
1472/3
*The Virgin and Child**
(p. 59)
oil on panel,
55.5×31.5 cm
1440–1445

CIGNANI, Carlo
Bologna, 1628—
Forli, 1719
The Fall of Man
oil on canvas,
312×197 cm
mature work

**CIGOLI, Lodovico
Cardi da**
Castelvecchio/Empoli,
1559—Rome, 1613
The Virgin and Child
oil on canvas,
85×70.5 cm
early work

**CIPPER, Giacomo
Francesco (Todeschini)**
in Northern Italy,
1705–1736
*Young Peasant Couple with
Musicians*
oil on canvas,
103.5×169 cm

CLAESZ, Pieter
Burg-Steinfurt, 1597/8—
Haarlem, 1660
Still-life
oil on panel,
63.6×88.3 cm
signed and dated 1647

**CLAUDE, Lorrain
(Claude Gellée)**
Chamagne/Mirecourt,
1600—Rome, 1682
*Villa in the Roman
Campagna** (p. 58)
oil on canvas,
68.8×91 cm
1640s
Landscape
wash and pastel,
22.3×32.9 cm
c. 1645

CLERCK, Hendrick de
before 1570—Brussels,
1630
Rest on the Flight to Egypt
oil on canvas,
137×108 cm
signed, 1590s

**CLEVE, Joos van
(Joos van der Beke)**
after 1480—Antwerp,

1540/1
*The Virgin and Child**
(p. 63)
oil on panel,
52.5×42 cm
1515–1520 (?)

**COCXIE, Michiel van
(Michiel van Coxie)**
Mechelen, 1497—1592
*Portrait of Christina,
Widow of the Duke
of Lorraine*
oil on panel,
35.3×27.5 cm

COELLO, Claudio
Madrid, 1630/5–1693
St. Dominic
oil on canvas,
201×127 cm
The Holy Family
oil on canvas,
248×169 cm
signed

COLOGNE Master
*St John the Evangelist**
(p. 98)
oak, 183 cm
late 15th century

COLOGNE Master
St Margaret
brush and pastel,
21.4×14 cm
c. 1400

COLOMBEL, Nicolas
Sotteville/Rouen, 1644—
Paris, 1717
Hagar and the Angel
oil on canvas,
73.5×97 cm

CONSTABLE, John
East Bergholt (Suffolk),
1776—London, 1837
*Waterloo Celebrations
at East Bergholt** (p. 91)
oil on canvas,
23×33.5 cm
The Dam
oil on canvas,
11.5×17 cm

COQUES, Gonzales
Antwerp, 1614–1684
A Family from Antwerp
oil on panel,
65,5×89.5 cm
1650s

**CORNELIS VAN
HAARLEM
(Cornelis Cornelisz.)**
Haarlem, 1562–1638
*The Golden Age
(Bacchanalia)*
oil on canvas,
157×193.5 cm
signed and dated 1614
The Judgement of Paris
oil on panel,
40×52 cm
signed and dated 1628

**COROT,
Jean-Baptiste Camille**
Paris, 1796–1875
Italian Landscape
oil on canvas,

36.3×28.3 cm
signed, *c.* 1826
*Woman with Daisies**
(p. 113)
oil on canvas, 78×58 cm
1868–1870
Souvenir de Coubron
oil on canvas,
46×55.3 cm
signed, 1872

**CORREGGIO
(Antonio Allegri)**
Correggio, 1489/94—
1534
*Virgin and Child with an
Angel (Madonna del Latte)**
(p. 37)
oil on panel,
68.5×56.8 cm
1520s
The Virgin
chalk drawing,
26.3×18.3 cm
c. 1520

COSTA, Lorenzo
Ferrara, *c.* 1460—
Mantua, 1535
*Venus** (p. 36)
oil on panel,
174×76 cm
*The Holy Family with
St Jerome and St Francis*
oil on panel, 88×72 cm
signed, early 16th century

COTER, Colyn de
active in Brussels and
Antwerp, late 15th and
early 16th centuries
St John the Evangelist
transferred from panel to
canvas, 113×75 cm
Mary Magdalene
oil on panel,
112×55.2 cm
companion piece of the
previous picture

COURBET, Gustave
Ornans, 1819—Latour-
de-Peilz, 1877
The Wrestlers
oil on canvas,
252×198 cm
signed and dated 1853
*Spring at Fouras** (p. 112)
oil on canvas,
62.5×81 cm
signed, 1863
Landscape with Pine Tree
oil on canvas,
81.5×101.5 cm
signed, 1868
The Lake of Neuchâtel
oil on canvas, 50×60 cm
signed, 1876

COUTURE, Thomas
Senlis, 1815—Villers-
le-Bel, 1879
Bird-catching
oil on canvas,
42×61 cm
signed and dated 1857

COZZARELLI, Guidoccio
Siena, 1450–1516
*The Virgin and Child
Enthroned with Saints*
tempera on panel,
166×137.5 cm
signed and dated 1486

Villabona, 1730
Faith, Hope and Charity
oil on canvas,
176×145.4 cm

LE BRUN, Charles
Paris, 1619–1690
*The Apotheosis of
Louis XIV*
oil on canvas,
109.5×78.3 cm
1677

LEIBL, Wilhelm
Cologne, 1844—
Würzburg, 1900
Pál Szinyei Merse
oil on canvas,
139×102 cm
1869

**LELY, Sir Peter
(Pieter van der Faes)**
Soest/Utrecht, 1618—
London, 1680
Portrait of Frances Stuart
oil on canvas,
235×140 cm

LENBACH, Franz von
Schrobenhausen, 1836—
Munich, 1904
*The Triumphal Arch of Titus
in Rome*
oil on canvas,
179×130 cm
signed and dated 1860

LEONARDO da Vinci
Vinci, 1452—Cloux, 1519
Heads of Warriors
pastel,
19.1×18.8 cm
1503–1504
*Warrior ("The Red Head")**
(p. 101)
pastel,
22.6×18.6 cm
1503–1504
*Equestrian Statue**
(p. 94)
bronze, 26.5 cm
1516–1519

LESUEUR, Eustache
Paris, 1616–1655
Juno
pastel,
28.2×39.5 cm
1652–1655

LIBALT, Gottfried
c. 1610—Vienna, 1673
Shot Fowl
oil on canvas,
116.6×168 cm
signed

LIBERALE da Verona
Verona, c. 1445—
1526/9
*The Virgin and Child with
an Angel*
tempera on panel,
66×46,4 cm

LIBERI, Marco
Padua, 1640—after 1725
Jupiter and Mnemosyne
oil on canvas,
118×153 cm
signed

LICINIO, Bernardino
Poscante, 1489—
Venice, before 1565
Portrait of a Woman
oil on panel, 90×75 cm

LIEVENS, Jan
Leyden, 1607—
Amsterdam, 1674
Portrait of a Girl
oil on canvas,
61.5×48 cm
early 1630s

LIPPI, Filippino
Prato, c. 1457—
Florence, 1504
*St Anthony of Padua
Commends a Friar to the
Patronage of the Virgin**
(p. 33)
tempera on panel,
57×41.5 cm
c. 1480

LISS, Johann (Jan Lys)
Oldenburg, c. 1590—
Venice, 1629
*Judith with the Head of
Holofernes**
(p. 52)
oil on canvas,
129×104 cm
Venetian period
*A Country Wedding
Procession*
oil on canvas,
65.5×81.5 cm
c. 1620

LOIR, Nicolas
Paris, 1624–1679
Cleobis and Biton
oil on canvas,
61×74 cm

LOO, Jean-Baptiste van
Aix-en-Provence, 1684—
1745
Apollo and Daphne
oil on canvas,
157×127.5 cm
1720–1737

LORENZETTI, Ambrogio
active in Central Italy,
1313–1348
Virgin and Child Enthroned
tempera on panel,
85×58 cm
c. 1330

LORENZO da Viterbo
Viterbo (?), 1437—after 1476
Christ Blessing
fresco, transferred to
canvas,
665×162 cm

LORENZO, Monaco
Siena (?), c. 1370—
Florence, 1425
Christ on the Cross
tempera on panel,
146×84 cm

**LORRAIN: see CLAUDE
Lorrain**

LOTTO, Lorenzo
Venice, c. 1480—
Loreto, 1556

*The Sleeping Apollo and
the Muses** (p. 44)
oil on canvas,
44.5×74 cm
c. 1545–1550
*Virgin and Child with
St Francis*
oil on canvas,
67.5×66 cm
late work

LUINI, Bernardino
Luino, c. 1480—
Milan, 1531/2
*Virgin and Child with
St Elizabeth and the Young
St John the Baptist*
transferred from panel
to canvas,
89×66 cm

**MACCHIETTI, Girolamo
(Del Crocefissaio)**
Florence, c. 1535–1592
*Virgin and Child with
St Anne** (p. 48)
oil on panel,
174×117 cm

MAES, Nicolas
Dordrecht, 1632—
Amsterdam, 1693
Christ before Pilate
oil on canvas,
216×174 cm
early work
Justus Criex
oil on canvas,
109×92 cm
signed and dated 1666

**MAGNASCO, Alessandro
(Lissandrino)**
Genoa (?), 1667–1749
Friars at Lunch
oil on canvas,
72.5×56.2 cm
late work

MAGNELLI, Alberto
Florence, 1888—
Paris, 1971
Embrace
oil on canvas,
60×73 cm
signed and dated 1944

MAKART, Hans
Salzburg, 1840—
Vienna, 1884
Nessus Carries off Deianeira
oil on canvas,
142.5×93 cm
signed, c. 1870

MAN, Cornelis de
Delft, 1621–1706
The Chess Players
oil on canvas,
97.5×85 cm
signed

MANET, Édouard
Paris, 1832–1883
*Lady with Fan** (p. 114)
oil on canvas,
90×113 cm
signed 1863
*Barricade** (p. 109)
watercolour,
46.2×32.5 cm
signed 1871

MANGLARD, Adrien
Lyon, 1695—Rome, 1760
River Scene
oil on canvas,
55×98 cm
signed

MARATTI, Carlo
Camerano, 1625—
Rome, 1713
*Hera Tells Aeolus to Destroy
the Trojan Fleet*
wash, pen-and-ink,
23.2×28.9 cm
1670–1680

**MARCHESI, Girolamo
Marchesi da Cotignola**
Cotignola, c. 1481—
Rome (?) c. 1550
The Lamentation
oil on panel, 90×77 cm
signed

**MARCO d'Oggiono: see
OGGIONO, Marco da**

MARÉES, Hans von
Elberfeld, 1837—
Rome, 1887
*Sketches for the Picture
"Idylls"*
pencil, 52.2× 41.7 cm
1873–1874

MARTÍNEZ, Juán
Narvas de San Yuan,
1942
Cushions
wood fibre,
160×150 cm
1977

MARZIALE, Marco
active in Verona and
Cremona, 1489–1507
The Lamentation
tempera on panel,
81.5×95.3 cm

**MARY MAGDALENE
LEGEND, Master of the**
active in Brussels, late
15th c. early 16th century
*Christ in the House
of Simon the Pharisee*
oil on panel,
87.5×70 cm
1515–1520
Queen Mary of Hungary
oil on panel,
33.2×24 cm
c. 1530

MASO di Banco
active in Florence,
1320–1353
*The Coronation of the
Virgin** (p. 27)
tempera on panel,
51.2×51.7 cm

**Master of LIFE OF THE
VIRGIN**
active in Cologne,
c. 1450–1500
The Virgin of Mercy
oil on panel,
129.5×65.5 cm
c. 1480

MATEJKO, Jan Aloysius

Cracow, 1838–1893
The Battle of Varna
oil on panel, 58×91 cm
signed and dated 1879

MATTEO di Giovanni
Borgo San Sepolcro,
c. 1430–1495
The Apostle St Bartholomew
tempera on panel,
80.5×48 cm
c. 1480

**MAULBERTSCH, Franz
Anton**
Langenargen (am Bodensee),
1724—Vienna, 1796
*The Holy Trinity** (p. 82)
oil on canvas,
62.5×33 cm
1780s
Rebecca at the Well
oil on canvas,
73×90.5 cm
early work
*The Apotheosis of
St Stanislas*
oil on canvas,
30.3×53.7 cm
1760s
Young Man in Plumed Hat
lead rod,
20.5×24 cm
c. 1754

**MAZZOLA BEDOLI,
Girolamo**
Parma, c. 1500–1569
*The Holy Family with
St Francis*
oil on panel,
90.5×65 cm
late 1530s

MAZZOLINO, Lodovico
c. 1480—Ferrara, 1528
Christ before Pilate
oil on panel,
45.3×38.5 cm

MEMLING, Hans
Seligenstadt/Frankfurt
am Main, c. 1433—Bruges,
1494
*Domestic Altar/The Bearing
of the Cross, The Cruci-
fixion, The Resurrection,
The Annunciation** (p. 61)
oil on panel,
56×63 cm,
58.2×27.4 cm
after 1491

MENGS, Anton Raphael
Aussig, 1728—Rome, 1779
The Holy Family
canvas, grisaille,
126.5×154.5 cm

MENZEL, Adolf von
Breslau, 1815—
Berlin, 1905
*Sermon in the Beech
Grove near Kösen*
oil on canvas, 71×58 cm
signed and dated 1868
Study Sheet
pencil,
12.8×20.6 cm
1892

MEYTENS, Martin van

Stockholm, 1695—
Vienna, 1770
Self-portrait
oil on canvas,
Self-portrait
oil on canvas,
65×50.2 cm
1740–1741

MICHELE, da Verona
Verona, 1470—after 1536
The Dead Christ with Angels
oil on panel,
109.5×98.7 cm

MICHELE, Pannonio
of Hungarian extraction;
active in Ferrara after
1415; died 1459 or 1464
*Thalia** (p. 30)
oil and tempera on panel,
136.5×82 cm
signed 1456–1459

MICHELOZZO Michelozzi
Florence (?), 1396–1472
*Madonna in a Shell-shaped
Niche** (p. 93)
terracotta, 77×55 cm
1430–1450

**MIGNARD, Pierre
(Mignard le Romain)**
Troyes, 1612—Paris, 1695
Clio
oil on canvas,
143.5×115 cm
signed and dated 1689

MIGNON, Abraham
Frankfurt am Main, 1640—
Wetzlar (?), 1679
*Flower-piece with Fish and
a Birds' Nest*
oil on canvas,
89×71.5 cm
signed

MILLET, Jean-François
Gruchy, 1814—
Barbizon, 1875
Maternal Cares
pastel, 29.7×21.5 cm
signed

**MOEYAERT,
Claes Cornelisz.**
Amsterdam, 1592/3–1655
*Joseph Selling Wheat
in Egypt*
oil on panel,
69.5×103 cm

MOLENAER, Jan Miense
Haarlem, c. 1610–1668
*St Peter's Denial of Christ**
(p. 71)
oil on canvas,
99.5×135 cm
signed and dated 1636
*A Merry Company before
a Tavern*
oil on canvas,
87.8×102 cm
signed
The Music Makers
oil on canvas,
63×46 cm
signed

MOMPER, Joos de
Antwerp, 1564–1635

Divine Service in a Cave
oil on panel,
53×74 cm

MONET, Claude
Paris, 1840—
Giverny, 1926
The Harbour at Trouville
oil on canvas,
54×65.7 cm
signed and dated 1870
Apple-trees in Blossom
oil on canvas,
64.3×81 cm
signed and dated 1879
*Fishing Boats** (p. 114)
oil on canvas,
73×92.5 cm
signed and dated 1886

**MONTAGNA,
Bartolommeo**
Orzinuovi/Brescia,
c. 1450—Vicenza, c. 1523
*Alfonso II, King of Naples,
Gives Niccolò Orsini
a Banner*
fresco transferred to
canvas,
269×467 cm

**MONTAGNANA,
Jacopo da**
Montagnana/Padua,
1440/3—
after 1499
Pietà
tempera on panel,
76×50.5 cm

**MORETTO da Brescia
(Alessandro Bonvicino)**
Brescia, c. 1498–1554
St Roch with an Angel
oil on canvas,
227×151 cm
1540s
A Martyr Saint
oil on canvas,
81×71.5 cm
(with inscription)

MORLAND, George
London, 1763–1804
The Pigsty
oil on canvas,
50.1×66 cm

**MORONI,
Giovanni Battista**
Albino/Bergamo, 1520/5—
Bergamo, 1578
*Jacopo Contarini(?)** (p. 45)
oil on canvas,
105×83.5 cm
signed 1575
(with inscription)

MURA, Francesco de
Naples, 1696–1782
The Virgin and Child
oil on canvas,
38×26.5 cm (oval)

**MURILLO,
Bartolomé Estéban**
Seville, 1618–1682
*The Infant Jesus
Distributing Bread to
Pilgrims** (p. 88)
oil on canvas,
219×182 cm

1678
The Flight into Egypt
oil on canvas,
155.5×125 cm
1660s
*The Holy Family with the
Young St John the Baptist*
oil on canvas,
156×126 cm
companion piece to the
previous work

NALDINI, Battista
Florence, 1537–1591
The Three Graces
oil on panel,
205×144 cm
The Crucifixion
oil on panel,
81.5×64 cm

NEER, Aert van der
Amsterdam, 1603/4–1677
Moonlit Landscape
oil on panel,
37×53 cm
signed

NERI di Bicci
Florence, 1419–1491
Madonna Enthroned
tempera on panel,
120×80.5 cm

NETSCHER, Caspar
Heidelberg, 1639—
The Hague, 1684
The Presentation of a Locket
oil on canvas,
62×67.5 cm
signed

NEYN, Pieter de
Leyden, 1597–1639
Sandy Path
oil on panel,
35×63.3 cm

**NICCOLÒ da Foligno
(Niccolò di Liberatore
di Giacomo di Mariano)**
Foligno, 1425/30–1502
St Bernadino of Siena
tempera on canvas,
134×72.5 cm
signed and dated 1497

NICCOLÒ di Buonaccorso
mentioned 1348—
Siena, 1388
The Annunciation (diptych)
tempera on panel,
57×24.5 cm (each)
1370s

**NICCOLÒ di Segna
di Buonaventura**
mentioned Siena,
1331—c. 1345
The Coronation of the Virgin
tempera on panel,
51.5×32 cm
early 1330s

NORTH-ITALIAN Painter
a) *Orsina de Grassi*
oil on canvas,
101.5×85 cm
16th century

NORTH-ITALIAN Painter
b) *Portrait of Vittoria
Farnese*

oil on panel,
80×61.5 cm
mid-16th century

**NUÑEZ DE VILLAVI-
CENCIO, Pedro**
Seville, 1644–1700
Spilt Apples
oil on canvas,
96.5×136.5 cm

OCHTERVELT, Jacob
Rotterdam 1634—
Amsterdam 1682
A Dutch Family
oil on canvas,
96.5×91 cm
signed and dated 1670

OGGIONO, Marco d'
Oggiono, c. 1475—
Milan, 1530
Angel with Censer
oil on panel,
114×47 cm

OPIE, John
St Agnes/Truro, 1761—
London, 1807
Portrait of a Woman
oil on canvas,
73.4×63 cm

**ORCAGNA: see JACOPO
di Cione**

ORLEY, Barend van
active in Brussels,
1525—died 1541
*The Emperor Charles V**
(p. 62)
oil on panel,
71.5×51.5 cm
late 1510s
Sharing the Game
wash, pen-and-ink,
38.7×53.7 cm
c. 1525

ORRENTE, Pedro
Monte Alegre, c. 1570/80—
Valencia, 1644
The Supper at Emmaus
oil on canvas,
81×101 cm

OSTADE, Adriaen van
Haarlem, 1610–1684
*The Fishwife** (p. 74)
oil on panel,
29×26.5 cm
c. 1672
Peasant Family
oil on panel,
43.1×36.5 cm
signed and dated 1647
Pen Sharpener
oil on panel,
33.2×26.7 cm
Dutch Peasant Family
wash, pen-and-ink,
23.8×19.4 cm
c. 1647–1648

OSTADE, Isaack van
Haarlem, 1621–1649
Pig-killing
oil on panel,
39.8×53.8 cm
signed and dated 1642

OVENS, Jürgen

Tönning, 1623—Friedrich-
stadt a. d. Eider, 1678
A Mother and Her Children
oil on canvas, 89×74 cm
signed and dated 1657

PACHER, Friedrich
Neustift/Brixen (?),
1435/40—
after 1508
Christ in Limbo
oil on panel,
130×95 cm
(including frame)
early work

**PALMA Giovane (Jacopo
di Antonio Palma)**
Venice, 1544–1626
*The Dead Christ with
Two Angels*
oil on canvas,
85×115.5 cm

**PALMA Vecchio (Jacopo
d'Antonio Nigretti)**
Serinalta/Bergamo,
c. 1480—Venice, 1528
Bust of a Youth
oil on panel,
38.7×29 cm
early work
Bust of a Girl
oil on panel,
38.8×28.5 cm
companion piece to
the previous panel

**PARMIGIANINO
(Francesco Mazzola)**
Parma, 1503—
Casal Maggiore, 1540
Shepherd and Shepherdess
wash, pen-and-ink,
21.3×20.5 cm
1524–1530

PAUDISS, Christoph (?)
Hamburg (?), c. 1618—
Freising, 1666
Kitchen Still-life
oil on panel,
53×71 cm

**PELLEGRINI,
Giovanni Antonio**
Venice, 1675–1741
*Christ Healing the Man
Stricken with Palsy*
oil on canvas,
95×50 cm
c. 1730

**PENNACCHI, Girolamo
(Girolamo da Treviso)**
Treviso, 1455–1497 (?)
Virgin and Child
tempera on panel,
68.2×50.7 cm

PEREDA, Antonio
Valladolid, 1611—
Madrid, 1678
*St Anthony of Padua Wor-
shipping the Infant Christ*
oil on canvas,
177×205 cm

**PETTENKOFEN,
August von**
Vienna, 1822–1889
Fair at Szolnok

oil on panel,
9×16 cm
signed and dated 1874

**PIAZZA DA LODI,
Martino**
died in Lodi, 1527
*Virgin and Child with the
Young St John the Baptist*
oil on panel,
32.3×23.9 cm
c. 1520

**PIERO DI COSIMO
(Piero de Lorenzo)**
Florence, 1462–1521
Christ on the Cross
oil on panel,
160×120.5 cm
early 16th century

**PIETRO DA MESSINA
(Pietro de Saliba)**
active in Messina, Genoa
and Venice 1497–1530
Christ at the Column
oil on panel,
35.5×29 cm
signed

**PINO, Marco dal
(Marco da Siena)**
Costa al Pino/Siena,
c. 1525—Naples, 1587/8
Ecce Homo
oil on panel,
165×101 cm

**PIOMBO, Sebastiano del
(Sebastiano Luciani)**
Venice, 1485—
Rome, 1547
*Portrait of a Man** (p. 42)
oil on panel,
115×94 cm
c. 1515
Portrait of a Girl
oil on panel,
52.5×42.8 cm
early work
Christ Bearing the Cross
oil on stone,
157×118 cm
late 1530s

PISANO, Andrea
Pontedera, *c.* 1290—
Orvieto, 1349
*Virgin and Child** (p. 92)
marble, 31 cm
1330–1336

PISSARRO, Camille
Saint Thomas, West Indies,
1831—Paris, 1903
La Varenne-de-Saint-Hilaire
oil on canvas,
49.6×74 cm
signed, *c.* 1863
*The Pont Neuf** (p. 115)
oil on canvas,
55×46.5 cm
signed and dated 1902

**PITTONI,
Giovanni Battista**
Venice, 1687–1767
*St Elizabeth of Hungary
Distributing Alms*
oil on canvas,
72×42.5 cm
c. 1734

The Nativity
oil on canvas,
38.5×46.5 cm
c. 1740

**POELENBURGH,
Cornelis van**
Utrecht, *c.* 1586–1667
*The Children of Elector
Palatine Frederic V,
King of Bohemia*
oil on panel,
37.9×65.3 cm
signed and dated 1628

**PONTE, Giovanni dal
(Giovanni di Marco)**
Florence, 1385—after 1437
*The Mystic Marriage of
St Catherine* and
*Episodes from the Legend
of St Catherine** (p. 29)
tempera on panel,
147×168.5 cm
23×50 cm
36×15 cm
1421 (with inscription)

PORCELLIS, Jan
Gent, *c.* 1584—
Soeterwoude/Leyden, 1632
Stormy Sea
oil on panel,
21.2×30.4 cm
signed

**PORDENONE, Giovanni
Antonio da (De Sacchi)**
Pordenone, 1483—
Ferrara, 1539
St Luke
oil on panel,
75×75 cm

POTTER, Paulus
Enkhuizen, 1625—
Amsterdam, 1654
*Landscape with a Shepherd
and a Shepherdess*
oil on panel,
67×114.5 cm
signed, early work

POUSSIN, Nicolas
Villers/Les Andelys
(Normandy) 1594—
Rome, 1665
*The Rest on the Flight
into Egypt*
oil on canvas,
57×74 cm
late 1620s

PREVITALI, Andrea
Bergamo, *c.* 1470–1528
The Virgin and Child
oil on panel,
68.7×53.2 cm
c. 1505

**PUVIS DE CHAVANNES,
Pierre**
Lyon, 1824—
Paris, 1898
*Mary Magdalene** (p. 117)
oil on canvas,
116.5×89.5 cm
signed and dated 1897

PYNACKER, Adam
Pynacker/Delft, 1621/2—
Amsterdam, 1673

*Rocky Landscape with
Waterfall*
oil on panel,
55×46 cm
late work

QUESNEL, Augustin
1595–1661
Woman Playing the Guitar
oil on panel,
34.5×26 cm
signed and dated 1635

**RAPHAEL (Raffaello
Santi)**
Urbino, 1483—Rome, 1520
*The Esterházy Madonna**
(p. 39)
tempera and oil on panel,
28.5×21.5 cm
1508
*Portrait of the Young
Pietro Bembo** (p. 38)
oil on panel, 54×39 cm
c. 1504–1506
Female Nude (Psyche)
metal rod drawing,
18.9×7.5 cm
1510–1515

RÉGNIER: see RENIERI

**REMBRANDT,
Harmensz. van Rijn**
Leyden, 1606—
Amsterdam, 1669
*The Dream of St Joseph**
(p. 73)
oil on canvas,
105×83 cm
c. 1650
The Old Rabbi
oil on panel,
70.5×53.5 cm
signed and dated 1642
The Slaughtered Ox
oil on panel, 53×44 cm
signed 1639 (false)
*Dutch Peasant Cottage**
(p. 106)
wash, pen-and-ink,
16.4×22.5 cm
1636
*Woman with Weeping Child
and Dog*
pen-and-ink,
18.2×14.5 cm
c. 1636
Saskia
wash, pen-and-ink,
16.3×12.5 cm
c. 1636

**REMBRANDT, Harmensz.
van Rijn and DOU,
Gerard**
*The Parable of the Hidden
Treasure*
oil on panel,
70.5×90 cm
c. 1630

**REMBRANDT, Harmensz.
van Rijn, Follower of**
Portrait of a Woman
oil on canvas, 82×65 cm

RENI, Guido
Bologna, 1575–1642
David and Abigail
oil on canvas,
153×161 cm

c. 1630
*Sketch for "The Crucifixion
of St Peter"*
wash, pen-and-ink,
22.9×13.8 cm
1601–1604

**RENIERI, Niccolò
(Nicolas Regnier)**
Maubeuge, *c.* 1590—
Venice, 1667
*Card-players** (p. 56)
oil on canvas,
174×228 cm
before 1626

RENOIR, Auguste
Limoges, 1841—
Cagnes, 1919
Portrait of a Girl
oil on canvas,
56.5×47 cm
signed 1900
After a Bath
pastel, 47.8×31.3 cm
signed 1894

REYNOLDS, Sir Joshua
Devonshire, 1723—
London, 1792
*Admiral Sir Edward
Hughes** (p. 91)
oil on canvas, 76×63 cm

**RIBERA, Jusepe de
(Lo Spagnoletto)**
Játiba, 1591—
Naples, 1652
*The Martyrdom of
St Andrew** (p. 86)
oil on canvas,
209×183 cm
signed and dated 1628

RIBOT, Théodule
St Nicolas d'Attes, 1823—
Colombes, 1891
Still-life
oil on canvas,
60×74.5 cm
signed *c.* 1865

RICCI, Sebastiano
Belluno, 1659—
Venice, 1734
*Bathsheba Bathing**
(p. 52) oil on canvas,
118.5×199 cm
1720s
*Moses Defending the
Daughters of Jethro*
oil on canvas,
114×178 cm
companion piece of the
previous canvas
The Assumption
oil on canvas,
95×51.5 cm
1733–1734
Venus and the Satyr
oil on canvas,
100.7×125.3 cm
late work

**RICCIO, Andrea
(Andrea Briosco)**
Padua, 1470–1532
*The Rape of Europa**
(p. 95)
bronze, 18.2 cm
mature period

RIGAUD, Hyacinthe
Perpignan, 1659—
Paris, 1743
Portrait of Cardinal Fleury
oil on canvas,
150.5×110 cm
after 1728

ROBERT, Hubert
Paris, 1733–1808
*Antique Ruins** (p. 57)
oil on panel,
32.8×24.8 cm
signed

ROCCA, Michele
Parma, 1670/5—after 1751
Samson and Delilah
oil on canvas,
44.5×34 cm

RODIN, Auguste
Paris, 1840–Meudon, 1917
Sketch of Madame Séverine
pastel, 32.1×27 cm
signed *c.* 1893

ROMAKO, Anton
Atzgersdorf, 1832—
Döbling, 1889
August Wassermann
oil on canvas,
106×76 cm
signed *c.* 1878

ROMANINO, Girolamo
Brescia, 1484/7—
1562 or after
*Madonna and Child** (p. 44)
oil on panel, 55×46 cm
Portrait of a Man
oil on panel,
82.5×71.5 cm
1520s

ROOS, Johann Heinrich
Otterberg (Pfalz), 1631—
Frankfurt am Main, 1685
*A Shepherd and His Family
at the Well*
oil on canvas,
75.5×92 cm
signed

**ROSA, Francesco de
(Pacecco)**
c. 1600—Naples, 1654
*Moses Brings Forth Water
Out of the Rock*
oil on canvas,
203×257.5 cm
early work

ROSA, Salvator
Arenella, 1615—
Rome, 1673
Seaport with Ruins
oil on canvas,
87.5×111 cm
signed

ROSSELLI, Matteo
Florence, 1578—1650
The Allegory of Fidelity
oil on canvas,
78×60.5 cm

ROSSETTI, Dante Gabriel
London, 1828—
Birchington-on-Sea, 1882
Study of a Head
pencil,
26.2×26.2 cm

ROTARI, Pietro
Verona, 1707—
St Petersburg, 1762
Girl with Distaff
oil on canvas,
48×39.2 cm

RUBENS, Sir Peter Paul
Siegen, 1577—
Antwerp, 1640
Study of a Man's Head
oil on panel, 55×42 cm
1617–1619

RUBENS, Sir Peter Paul and DYCK, Sir Anthony van
Mucius Scaevola before Porsenna* (p. 67)
oil on canvas,
187×156 cm
before 1621

RUISDAEL, Jacob van
Haarlem, 1628/9–1682
The View of Amsterdam*
(p. 77)
oil on canvas,
52.5×43.5 cm
signed, *c.* 1660
Forest Lake
oil on panel,
66×48.9 cm
early work

RUYSDAEL, Salomon van
Naarden, *c.* 1602—
Haarlem, 1670
Riverscape with Ferry
oil on canvas,
100×135 cm
signed and dated 1644
After the Rain
oil on panel,
56×86.5 cm
signed and dated 1631
Battle Scene with Cavalry
oil on canvas,
89.5×110.5 cm
signed and dated 1659
Inn with a Maypole
oil on canvas,
80.5×111 cm
signed and dated 1664

RYCKAERT III, David
Antwerp, 1612–1661
A Merry Company
oil on canvas,
92.5×77.5 cm
signed
The Adoration of the Shepherds
oil on canvas,
88.5×119 cm

SACCHETTI, Lorenzo
Padua, 1759—
Pilsen, 1829
Antique Ruins (set design)
brush drawing,
39.8×25.2 cm

SAENREDAM, Pieter Jansz.
Assendelft, 1597—
Haarlem, 1665
The Interior of the Nieuwe Kerk in Haarlem* (p. 75)
oil on panel,
86×103 cm
signed and dated 1653

SÁNCHEZ, Pedro
active 1450–1500
The Entombment
tempera on panel,
82×90 cm
signed

SANO, di Pietro (Ansano di Pietro di Mencio)
Siena, 1406–1481
The Dance of Salome
tempera on panel,
23.5×33 cm

SANSOVINO, Jacopo (Jacopo Tatti)
Florence, 1486—
Venice, 1570
Madonna and Child* (p. 95)
wax and stucco-covered
linen applied on
a wooden
core, gilded, 63 cm
c. 1515–1518

SANTI, Giovanni
Colbordolo, 1430/40—
Urbino, 1494
The Risen Christ* (p. 35)
transferred from panel to
canvas, 66.5×54.5 cm
School of SANTI, Giovanni
*Madonna Enthroned
with Saints*
tempera and oil on panel,
172×142 cm
dated (July 2) 1488

SASSETTA (Stefano di Giovanni)
Siena, *c.* 1392—*c.* 1450
*St Thomas Aquinas before
the Altar of the Virgin** (p. 29)
tempera on panel,
23.6×39 cm
1423–1426

SAVERY, Roelandt Jacobsz.
Courtrai, 1576—
Utrecht, 1639
*Landscape with Lion
Lacerating a Cow*
oil on canvas,
97.5×135 cm
signed and dated 1628

SCARSELLA, Ippolito (Lo Scarsellino)
Ferrara, 1551–1620
*The Mystic Marriage of
St Catherine*
oil on panel,
50×34.2 cm

SCHMIDT, Martin Johann (Kremserschmidt)
Grafenwörth/Krems, 1718—
Stein/Krems, 1801
The Judgement of Solomon
canvas stretched on panel,
29×44 cm
1781
Esther and Ahasuerus
pen-and-ink pastel,
38.6×30.9 cm
1770s

SCHÖNFELD, Johann Heinrich
Biberach/Riss, 1609—

Augsburg, *c.* 1682
Aeneas and Anchises
oil on canvas,
229×154 cm

SEGANTINI, Giovanni
Arco, 1858—
Schafberg, 1899
The Angel of Life* (p. 118)
cardboard,
59.5×47.9 cm
signed, 1894

SELLAIO, Jacopo del
Florence 1441/2–1493
Esther before Ahasuerus
tempera on panel, 45×43 cm
St John the Baptist
tempera on canvas,
157×79.5 cm

SEYBOLD, Christian
Mainz, 1697—
Vienna, 1768
*Laughing Man with Black
Pudding*
oil on canvas,
70.3×60.3 cm
signed and dated 1760

SEVERINI, Gino
Cortona, 1883—
Paris, 1966
*Portrait of the
Artist's Wife*
oil on canvas,
100×73 cm
signed, *c.* 1935

SHISHKIN, Ivan Ivanovich
Jelabuga, 1831—
St Petersburg, 1898
Woodland Scene
cardboard, 37.5×24 cm
signed, *c.* 1875

SIBERECHTS, Jan
Antwerp, 1627—
London, 1703 (?)
The Ford
oil on canvas,
71.8×59.6 cm
signed and dated 1672

SIGNAC, Paul
Paris, 1863–1935
Riverside
watercolour,
25.7×40.4 cm
signed and dated 1900

SIGNORELLI Luca's workshop of
Cortona, 1441(?)–1523
Tiberius Gracchus
oil on panel,
107×51.5 cm
(with inscription)

SITTOW, Michel (Miguel Zittoz, Miguel el Flamenco)
Reval/Tallinn, 1469–
1525
The Virgin and Child
oil on panel,
33.8×24 cm
1490s

SLEVOGT, Max
Landshut, 1868—

Neukastel, 1932
Still-life with Flowers
oil on canvas, 51×61 cm
signed and dated 1921

SNYDERS, Frans
Antwerp, 1579–1657
Still-life
wash, pen-and-ink,
18.7×26.4 cm

SODOMA (Giovanni Antonio Bazzi)
Vercelli, *c.* 1477—
Siena, 1549
The Scourging of Christ
oil on panel,
36.5×70.3 cm
1510s
The Death of Lucretia
oil on panel,
71×61 cm

SOLIMENA, Francesco
Canale di Serino,
1657—Barra, 1747
*The Martyrdom of
St Placidus and Flavia*
oil on canvas,
75×153 cm
1700–1702

SOUTH GERMAN Master
Madonna and Child* (p. 96)
limestone, 120 cm
c. 1420–1430

SOUTH TYROLESE Master
Calvary Group* (p. 97)
painted lime,
38, 27.5, 29.5 cm
c. 1430

SPANZOTTI, Giovanni Martino
before 1456–1526/28
Pietà
tempera on panel,
66.5×47 cm
c. 1500

SPINELLO, Aretino (Spinello di Luca Spinelli)
Arezzo, *c.* 1352–1410
*St Nemesius and
St John the Baptist**
(p. 28)
tempera on panel,
139×86.5 cm (each)
194×94.5 cm (with frame)
1385 (with inscription)

SPRANGER, Bartholomäus
Antwerp, 1546—
Prague, 1611
Diana
oil on canvas,
69.2×52 cm

STEEN, Jan
Leyden, 1626–1679
*A Merry Company
(The Cat Family)** (p. 74)
oil on canvas,
150×148 cm
signed, 1670s
Courtesan
oil on panel,
61.6×46 cm
signed

STELLA, Jacques
Lyon, 1596—
Paris, 1657
*The Betrothal of
the Virgin*
oil on canvas,
108×140 cm

STEVENS, Alfred
Brussels, 1823—
Paris, 1906
Woman Playing the Harp
oil on canvas,
79.6×57 cm
signed, *c.* 1870

STROZZI, Bernardo
Genoa, 1581—
Venice, 1644
The Tribute Money* (p. 50)
oil on canvas,
158×225 cm
after 1631
The Annunciation
oil on canvas,
145×120 cm
Venetian period
The Annunciation
oil on canvas,
62.5×32 cm
Venetian period

STUCK, Franz von
Tettenweis, 1863—
Tetschen, 1928
Spring
oil on panel,
70.4×68.5 cm
signed and dated 1902

TADDEO di Bartolo
1362/3–1422
Madonna dell'Umiltà
tempera on panel,
114×72 cm
signed and dated 1395
(with inscription)

TEMPEL, Abraham van den
Leuwarden, 1622—
Amsterdam, 1672
Portrait of a Married Couple
oil on canvas,
119×156 cm

TENIERS THE YOUNGER, David
Antwerp, 1610—
Brussels, 1690
The Barber-Surgeon's Shop
oil on panel, 46×63 cm
signed and dated, 1636
A Game of Tric-trac
oil on panel,
25×35 cm
signed

The Circle of TERBRUGGHEN, Hendrick
Deventer, 1588—
Utrecht, 1629
The Calling of St Matthew
oil on canvas,
106×128 cm

TIEPOLO, Giovanni Battista
Venice, 1696—Madrid, 1770
*St James the Greater
Conquers the Moors** (p. 54)

Oil on canvas,
317×163 cm
signed, *c.* 1759
The Virgin with Six Saints
oil on canvas,
72.8×56 cm
late 1750s
Study of a Figure
pastel,
39.2×22.8 cm
c. 1752

TIEPOLO,
Giovanni Domenico
Venice, 1727–1804
The Rest on the Flight
into Egypt
oil on canvas,
47.7×65 cm
The Head of St James
the Greater* (p. 102)
pastel, 32.2×25.3 cm
c. 1760

TINTORETTO
(Jacopo Robusti)
Venice, 1518–1594
Hercules Expelling the Faun
from Omphale's Bed*
(p. 45)
oil on canvas,
112×106 cm
late work
The Supper at Emmaus
oil on canvas,
156×212 cm
1540–1545
Portraid of a Young Woman
oil on canvas,
38×33.3 cm
c. 1550
Studies of a Model Statuette*
(p. 102)
pastel, 27.6×27.2 cm
1547–1557

TITIAN
(Tiziano Vecellio)
Pieve di Cadore,
c. 1489—Venice, 1576
Portrait of the Doge
Marcantonio Trevisani*
(p. 43)
oil on canvas,
100×86.5 cm
after 1553
Portrait of Cardinal
Pietro Bembo
oil on canvas,
57.5×45.5 cm

TOULOUSE-LAUTREC,
Henri de
Albi, 1864—
Malromé, 1901
Ces Dames
cardboard, 60.3×80.5 cm
signed, 1895

TOURNIÈRES, Robert
Caen, 1667–1752
Count Ferdinand Adolf von
Plettenberg and His Family
oil on canvas,
92×74 cm
signed and dated 1727

TRECK, Jan Jansz.
c. 1606–1652
Still-life with Pewter Jug
oil on panel,
66.5×50.5 cm
signed and dated, 1645

TREVISANI, Francesco
Capodistria, 1656—
Rome, 1747
Lucretia
oil on canvas,
100×74.5 cm

TRISTÁN, Luis
Toledo(?), 1586(?), 1624
The Adoration of the Magi
oil on canvas,
232×115 cm
signed and dated, 1620

TROYON, Constantin
Sèvres, 1810—
Paris, 1865
Cowherd
oil on canvas,
77×103 cm
signed, *c.* 1860

TUSCAN Master
Christ on the Cross
tempera on panel,
40.5×28.5 cm
(including frame)
late 13th century

UHDE, Fritz von
Wolkenburg, 1848—
Munich, 1911
The Sermon on the Mount
oil on canvas,
261×229 cm
signed *c.* 1886

UMBRIAN Painter
Allegorical Female Figures
(Strength, Justice
and Activity)
fresco,
315×70 cm
(each)
early 15th century

UTRILLO, Maurice
Paris, 1883—Dax, 1955
The Street
oil on canvas,
60×73 cm
signed, *c.* 1930

VACCARO, Andrea
Naples, 1604–1670
St Sebastian and
the Holy Woman
oil on canvas,
157.5×130 cm
signed

VAGA, Pierino del
Florence, 1501—
Rome, 1547
St Peter and St Paul
pen-and-ink,
26.3×29.1 cm

VALCKENBROCH,
Frederick van
Antwerp, *c.* 1570—
Nuremberg, 1623
Pilgrims Outside
a Forest Chapel
oil on canvas,
131.5×128.5 cm

VANNI, Francesco
Siena, *c.* 1563–1610
The Holy Family
oil on canvas,
97×83.5 cm

VASARELY, Victor
(Győző Vásárhelyi)
b. Pécs, 1908
Marsan
oil on canvas,
195×114 cm
signed, 1962

VEERENDAEL,
Nicolaes van
Antwerp, 1640–1691
The Bust of the Virgin in
a Garland
oil on canvas,
116.5×85.5 cm

VELÁZQUEZ, Diego
Rodríguez de Silva y
Seville, 1599—
Madrid, 1660
Peasants Having a Meal*
(p. 85)
oil on canvas,
96×112 cm
c. 1618

VELÁZQUEZ,
Workshop of
The Infanta Margaret
Theresa
oil on canvas,
121×107 cm

VELDE, Jan Jansz. van de
Haarlem, 1619/20—
Enkhuizen (?), 1662
Still-life* (p. 75)
oil on panel,
43.4×32.4 cm
signed

VELDE THE YOUNGER,
Willem van de
Leyden, 1633—
Greenwich, 1707
Warships on a Calm Sea
oil on canvas,
50×66.4 cm
signed and dated 1653

VERMEER
THE ELDER, Jan
Haarlem, 1628–1691
Haarlem from the
Overveen Dunes
oil on canvas,
77.5×101 cm

VERNET, Joseph
Avignon, 1714—
Paris, 1789
Landscape with Castle Ruins
oil on canvas,
48×64 cm

VERONESE Artist
The Initial M with
the Annunciation* (p. 102)
miniature painted on
pergamen,
13.8×15.2 cm
c. 1440–1450

VERONESE, Paolo
(Paolo Caliari)
Verona, 1528—
Venice, 1588
Portrait of a Man* (p. 46)
oil on canvas,
120×102 cm
early work
The Crucifixion

oil on canvas,
149×90 cm
before 1580
Peter of Amiens before the
Doge Michele Vital
wash, pen-and-ink,
14×27.3 cm
1576–1577

VERROCCHIO,
Andrea del
Florence, 1435—
Venice, 1488
Virgin and Child Enthroned
with Five Saints and Two
Angels* (p. 31)
tempera on panel,
168×177.5 cm
after 1461

VERSPRONCK,
Jan Cornelisz.
Haarlem, 1597–1662
Portrait of a Man
oil on canvas,
84.2×67.2 cm
signed and dated 1641

VIANEN, Paulus van
Utrecht, *c.* 1570—
Prague, 1613
River Landscape with Rafts*
(p. 107)
pen-and-ink, brush
drawing, 19.7×29.7 cm
1601–1603

VICTORS, Jan
Amsterdam, *c.* 1620—the
East Indies, after 1676
Abraham Sends Hagar Away
oil on canvas,
131×157.5 cm

VIVARINI,
Alvise and Workshop
Venice, 1445/6—*c.* 1503/5
The Virgin and Child with
St John the Baptist and
St Jerome
tempera on panel,
83.3×73.3 cm
signed and dated, 1496

VLIEGER, Simon de
Rotterdam, *c.* 1601—
Weesp, 1653
Ships on a Calm Sea
oil on panel, 60×83 cm
signed, *c.* 1650
Landscape with River
and Trees
oil on panel, 70×61 cm
signed
Hunters at the Well
oil on panel,
47.5×40 cm
signed

VOS, Cornelis de
Hulst, 1585—
Antwerp, 1651
A Family Portrait
oil on panel,
133×155 cm
signed (unfinished)

VOUET, Simon
Paris, 1590–1649
Apollo and the Muses* (p.
56)
oil on panel,
80×221.5 cm

Workshop of VOUET,
Simon
Sleeping Venus
oil on canvas,
100.5×84 cm

VRANCX, Sebastian
Antwerp, 1573–1647
Banquet in a Garden
oil on panel,
91×126 cm
signed

WALDMÜLLER,
Ferdinand Georg
Vienna, 1793–1865
The Peep-show* (p. 110)
oil on panel,
76×92.5 cm
signed and dated, 1847

WATTEAU, Jean-Antoine
Valenciennes, 1684—
Nogent-sur-Marne, 1721
Sketch Sheet* (p. 107)
pastel,
24.2×33.7 cm
1711

WEENIX, Jan Baptist
Amsterdam, 1621—
Doetinchem, before 1663
The Ruins of the Temple
of Vespasian in Rome
oil on canvas,
80.5×68.3 cm
signed

WERFF, Adriaen van der
Kralinger-Ambacht, 1659—
Rotterdam, 1722
Susanna in Her Bath
oil on panel,
41.5×32.5 cm

WESTPHALIAN Master
Virgin and Child with
Six Angels* (p. 59)
oil on panel,
68.2×59 cm
c. 1420

WILDENS, Jan
Antwerp, 1584/6–1653
Landscape with Farm*
(p. 69)
oil on canvas,
85.5×120.5 cm
signed, 1629 (?)

WINKLER EPITAPH,
Master of the
active in Vienna,
1450–1500
The Martyrdom of St John
the Evangelist
oil on panel,
87×74.2 cm

WITTE, Emanuel de
Alkmaar, 1617—
Amsterdam, 1692
Interior of the Oude Kerk
in Amsterdam
oil on panel,
63.5×52 cm

WOENSAM, Anton
Worms, late 15th century—
Cologne, 1541
The Crucifixion
oil on panel,